How to Fix Your Academic Writing Trouble

How to Fix Your Academic Writing Trouble

A practical guide

Inger Mewburn, Katherine Firth and Shaun Lehmann

Open University Press

Open University Press
McGraw-Hill Education
8th Floor, 338 Euston Road
London
England
NW1 3BH

and Two Penn Plaza, New York, NY 10121-2289, USA

First published 2019

Commissioning Editor: Vivien Antwi
Editorial Assistant: Karen Harris
Content Product Manager: Ali Davis

A catalogue record of this book is available from the British Library

ISBN-13: 9780335243327
ISBN-10: 0335243320
eISBN: 9780335243334

Library of Congress Cataloging-in-Publication Data
CIP data applied for

Typeset by Transforma Pvt. Ltd., Chennai, India
Printed and bound by CPI Group (UK) Ltd, Croydon, CR0 4YY

Praise page

Contents

List of tables   ix

List of figures   x

Acknowledgements   xi

1   INTRODUCTION: YOU MAY HAVE ACADEMIC WRITING TROUBLES,
    BUT YOU CAN FIX THEM!   1
    1.1 Why you should buy this book   1
    1.2 Time management for academic writing: the Pomodoro
         Technique, Shut Up and Write, and boot camps   7

2   'YOUR WRITING DOESN'T SOUND VERY ACADEMIC': HOW TO
    CONVINCE YOUR READER YOU BELONG   12
    2.1 How to unlearn high school English   13
    2.2 'This sounds chatty or not scholarly': getting
         the academic tone right   16
    2.3 'Who are you standing with?': being argumentative in
         your writing   18
    2.4 Getting beyond 'descriptive' writing by entering the
         theory wars   21
    2.5 Using verbs to signal you belong, plus a verb cheat sheet   24
    2.6 How to use references to show who your academic
         network is (and isn't)   28
    2.7 Using references as magic tokens to power up your writing   30
    2.8 'Do you really need all this detail?': how and when to
         use footnotes and appendices   32

3   'WHERE'S YOUR EVIDENCE FOR THIS?': USING WHAT YOU KNOW
    TO MAKE A CASE   37
    3.1 How to understand how different disciplines use evidence
         (and take advantage of it)   38
    3.2 How to move from having a research question to having
         an answer in your writing   41
    3.3 The almost invisible structure of paragraphs   44
    3.4 What is a warrant?: and how to use warrants to persuade
         your reader   47
    3.5 Signposting words: using conjunctive adverbs like
         'however' correctly   49
    3.6 Using figures to help and not hinder   52

4 'YOUR WRITING DOESN'T FLOW': MAKING YOUR TEXT COHERENT
AND FLUENT   58

    4.1 How to make sure your reader will understand what you are
        trying to say   59
    4.2 How to write a clear sentence   62
    4.3 Use signposting to guide academic readers   67
    4.4 Keep your sentences moving forward with themes and rhemes   69
    4.5 Untangling your tenses   72
    4.6 How to use free or generative writing to make progress
        (and create flow)   75
    4.7 Planning your writing with flexible techniques   79
    4.8 Solving illogical structures with reverse outlines   86

5 'WAFFLE': IMPROVING READABILITY BY MANAGING YOUR EXTRA WORDS   89

    5.1 Writing one whole sentence at a time   90
    5.2 How and when to use the passive voice   92
    5.3 How to kill zombie words   95
    5.4 Are you suffering from parataxis or hypotaxis?   97
    5.5 Fighting weeds and cutting your word count   99
    5.6 Get rid of filler words   101

6 'UNCRITICAL!': TAKING A STAND IN YOUR WRITING   105

    6.1 Who am I to question?   105
    6.2 Can I use 'I'?   109
    6.3 How not to be unintentionally exclusionary in your writing   112
    6.4 Avoiding excessive cleverness   116
    6.5 Hedging and boosting language   119
    6.6 Argument diagramming   122
    6.7 How to be more logical   130

7 'WHERE'S YOUR DISCUSSION SECTION?': STRUCTURING
YOUR WORK AS A WHOLE   134

    7.1 Designing your dissertation as a whole work   135
    7.2 Turning an annotated bibliography on steroids into a
        proper literature review   138
    7.3 Making and using a literature review matrix   141
    7.4 How to write an abstract   144
    7.5 How to write a good glossary   148
    7.6 Structuring multidisciplinary work   151

8 THE END OF THIS BOOK, BUT NOT THE END OF YOUR DISSERTATION   154

Notes   156

References   158

Index   161

Tables

2.1	Shaun's table of examples for choosing Latinate or Germanic academic terms	17
2.2	A verb cheat sheet	27
3.1	Table of epistemological (knowledge) differences between disciplines	40
3.2	Interdisciplinary methods from Katherine's PhD	40
3.3	When to use a conjunctive adjective, and how to know it's the right choice	51
4.1	Tense choice	73
4.2	Making a thesis map	82
4.3	Turning snowflake outline points into a dissertation structure	85
6.1	Critique table	107
6.2	Hedging phrases example 1	122
6.3	Hedging phrases example 2	122
7.1	Literature review matrix	143
7.2	Identifying the audiences for Inger's dissertation	150

Figures

3.1 Frequency histogram of housing values for a hypothetical
    city area   54
3.2 Frequency histogram of housing values for a hypothetical
    city area   55
3.3 Boxplot of house values for a hypothetical city area   56
3.4 Violin plot of values for a hypothetical city area   56
4.1 Start the spider diagram with a question or statement   80
4.2 Develop the spider diagram by filling in further questions   80
4.3 Snowflake outlines   81
4.4 Snowflake outlines: start with a triangle   83
4.5 Snowflake outlines: your triangle becomes a star   83
4.6 Snowflake outlines: your star becomes a rough ice crystal   84
4.7 Your outlined snowflake is now beautiful   84
5.1 Katherine's writing cycle   92
6.1 Example argument spider diagram on a whiteboard   123
6.2 Two-part argument diagram   124
6.3 The argument diagram now has two premises   125
6.4 Alternative hypothesis argument diagram   126
6.5 Spider diagram with alternative hypothesis developed
    through serial argument map   127
6.6 Completing the alternative hypothesis, mapped though
    spider diagrams, with linked argument map   128
6.7 Bringing both sides of the argument together in a
    spider diagram   129
7.1 Why chapters are not quite like content 'buckets'   136
7.2 A Venn diagram of audiences for Inger's dissertation   150

Acknowledgements

The examples we share at the beginning of each chapter were contributed by readers of our blogs and the Thesis Whisper social media gang, who also voted for the cover, gave us advice and cheered us on. Thank you. Our thanks also to all our students over many years who shaped and inspired every word of this book. We want to thank our own supervisors, and our colleagues, mentors and heroes, who have taught us so much that we now pass on to you. We are grateful to Karen Harris and the Open University Press team for making this book a real thing – and a thing of beauty. Earlier versions of chapters in this book appeared on the Thesis Whisperer blog, and Research Degree Voodoo Insiders blog.

On a personal note:

Inger says: Thanks to my son Brendan, who kindly allowed me to test out sections of this book on him. And to my husband Luke, for quietly placing cups of coffee at my elbow when I worked on the weekend. Love you both.

Katherine says: With thanks to the Thesis Boot Camp musketeers Liam and Peta, and to Andreas for being the co-author who let me test out sections of the book on him, and the partner who took me out to dinner when the editing got hard. Go team!

Shaun would like to thank Inger and Katherine for the opportunity to work on this book and for all of the things he learned from them in the process. He'd also like to acknowledge his colleagues at the ANU for their encouragement and ideas. Finally, he'd like to thank all of the students with whom he has worked over the years – without them it would be very hard to know which techniques for writing are of genuine worth.

1 Introduction: you may have academic writing troubles, but you can fix them!

1.1 Why you should buy this book

This book is designed to help you take competent 'student' writing and make it into mature 'academic' prose that will surprise and delight your advisors, examiners and colleagues.

Academics read a lot of tortured text written by their students. Some of this writing is technically competent, but for a range of reasons fails to persuade a highly knowledgeable and experienced reader. This book will help you please a reader who has extremely high standards of detail, quality and accuracy. Academics have high standards regarding content and writing style, but the style issues are often hidden under comments about content. Writing in an 'academic style' that makes you sound scholarly is essential, but it's easy to find yourself lost and confused if no one ever tells you there is a style, or how to achieve it.

This book puts the skill of 'writing like an academic' front and centre. We aim to help you 'pass' as an academic, even if you don't feel you are one – yet. We offer this advice with frankly pragmatic motives. Using the correct academic style for your discipline is crucial to passing your PhD examination.

This book is mostly written for doctoral students writing a full-length dissertation in English. We cover Science, Humanities and Creative disciplines, and give advice for traditional and innovative dissertation genres. Some of you may have picked this book up while you are doing your minor thesis or dissertation – great! What you hold in your hands is not really a beginner's book, although we hope beginners will get value out of it.

We have written this book for someone who can already write reasonably well but is looking for help (there's a reason you picked up a book with the word 'trouble' so plainly in the title!). You might be getting feedback that your writing is terrible, but you don't know why – or you might be expecting praise for your writing and not getting any. Even if you are quite a good writer, there is a lot to learn from this book – we all learned a lot from each other writing it!

Academic writing has a bit of a reputation problem: often characterised as impenetrable nonsense that has no connection to the 'real world'. While this criticism is a little unfair, it's not exactly untrue. Academic writing is full of 'insider language' that is hard for outsiders – and beginners – to decode.

Academics have a very different set of standards from the rest of the world. The demands of academic texts mean that some academics write prose they don't want to read! However, for an academic, being correct, concise and precise is more important than being fun to read. We want to make it possible for you to write prose that is clear, concise and legible – to academics.

When you are a student, it is wise to emulate your academic advisors, not innovate. While we have sympathy with critics like Helen Sword and Stephen Pinker, who argue academics should change the way they write, we acknowledge that students are not empowered to be the change these writers want to see. We take issue with advice books which encourage student writers to employ 'plain English', as this advice is unlikely to help you pass scrutiny by an academic reader steeped in their discipline traditions. Adapting advice that is designed to produce texts you see in the newspaper or magazines will lead you in the wrong direction. Accessible, reader-friendly, jargon-free writing is good for email and basic reports, but writing 'plain English' does not make you sound like a scholar.

Academic text is different from other genres for reasons that are historical, cultural and practical. Most people do not grow up with knowledge of how to write in an academic style, nor are they explicitly taught how to do it. We want to help you produce writing that is more like those complex academic texts with the aim of ensuring your ideas are taken seriously within academia.

If you have picked up this book, it's because the feedback you are getting on your writing is making you more confused, not less. We understand. We are experts in helping people to write 'like an academic'. People like us exist in all universities because many academics are subject matter experts who can write well, but haven't been trained to teach others to write. There is a gap between their expert doing and their ability to explain how (and why) they write the way they do.

When an academic doesn't know how to explain what is wrong with your writing, they will often add comments to your text just like the chapter headings in this book: 'your writing doesn't flow', or 'you don't sound very academic'. These phrases make perfect sense to experienced writers, but are often impenetrable to novices. To make matters worse, academics might not even realise they are not competent writing teachers.

Academics are accustomed to being, if not the smartest person in the room, one of the smartest people in their field. When they are not the smartest person, some academics are no longer sure who they are. People react in different ways to this feeling of uncertainty. Some throw their hands up and send you to people like us who do know how to teach writing. Some are arrogant and dismissive – and blame the student for being a 'bad writer'.

The worst types of advisor, in our opinion, are the ones who spend all their time 'fixing' your grammar, and thus avoid (consciously or unconsciously) engaging with the substance of your ideas. Some academics are so offended by stylistic errors, they refuse to engage with the content until the writing is already 'scholarly'. The error-spotting advisor may tell you exactly where you are wrong and what the text should be like, but be frustratingly vague on how to get there. All these reactions leave students feeling bewildered and demoralised.

We know how frustrating, eccentric and inadequate feedback is because we have been there ourselves. Between us, we have over 30 years' experience working with people just like you. It was our recognition of the gap between knowing how to write 'like an academic' and knowing how to teach it that motivated us to write this book in the first place. We are all academics involved with helping people write at a high level within a university context, from undergraduate to PhD and beyond. We wanted this book on our shelves to help our students, but we also wanted to help our academic colleagues. We know they are frustrated by the drafts they get from students, but also frustrated by not being sure how to tell students to fix it.

Taking your writing from good, technically competent prose to great academic writing is not easy, as evidenced by the plethora of books already on the market. Usually, these books suggest you start at the very beginning and proceed from there. This is great advice if you read them before you run into trouble, which we know many people do not.

This book is different. Our starting point is after you have already been given feedback. We start with typical feedback that advisors often write on the margins of your essays and chapter drafts. We help you diagnose what might have prompted the advisor to give you this feedback in the first place. Once you know what the problem might be, you can use one of our many strategies to try and fix it. *How to Fix Your Academic Writing Trouble* is a recipe book as much as it is a 'how to' manual. There is usually more than one reason why your writing gets poor feedback and multiple ways you can fix it. Alternatively, you may use this book to have a more informed conversation with your advisor, examiners or mentors. You might even be that advisor who doles out frustrating advice, if so – welcome! We are here to help.

It took us almost a year to settle on the format of this book because we wanted the reading experience to be like a cookery book for academic writers. We have arranged the book based on the most common types of feedback we have seen. You can skip straight to the chapter that seems to have the most promising 'recipe' to fix the writing trouble you are facing. Feel free to do that now. We do recommend you come back to read on in this introductory section, where we explain why you are in all kinds of writing trouble in the first place.

From mimicry to mastery

Learning to write 'like an academic' is about becoming a certain kind of expert writer. As Kamler and Thompson (2014) remind us, text work is identity work. Becoming an expert academic writer is inseparable from the process of becoming an academic. Eventually, your own, distinctive 'academic voice' must become legible to other members of your discipline community. If you do this correctly, your academic mentors will recognise and embrace you as one of their own. If you don't use similar words, in similar ways, with similar patterns of grammar and referencing, you will not 'sound academic enough', and your ideas will not be taken seriously by the people you want to impress.

Learning to write like an academic is a process that has distinct phases. Dreyfus and Dreyfus (1980) argue, there are five progressive stages we go through when acquiring any new skill: (1) Novice; (2) Advanced beginner; (3) Competent performer; (4) Proficient performer; and (5) Expert performer. In some areas of life, it is relatively easy to transition from novice to expert performer. Driving a car is a good example: once you have mastered a few basics, the best way to get better is to drive – a lot. The path from novice writer to expert academic writer is much more complicated.

When you were a novice writer, you learnt a bunch of objective facts – like spelling, grammar, how to hold a pen correctly. You probably spent a long time writing out rows and rows of the same letter until your teacher thought you had the shape right. You might have learned to type more or less the same way, by banging on a keyboard until your fingers 'knew' where to go. This context-free repetition ingrained basic writing know-how; you no longer think about how to write words into sentences, you just do it. The challenge at the next level, and beyond, is to make these sentences have meaning and persuade the reader to take up your point of view.

As you progress up the levels of expertise, the audience for your writing matters more and more. Academic writing is different from learning to be a journalist or novelist, and quite different to the basic skills of writing exam essays, reports or memos which you were (hopefully) taught in high school. It is the failure to pick up on the right academic context and respond to it adequately that leaves many students stuck at the 'competent performer' level of the Dreyfus' framework. When we reach this level, we know all the elements of writing and have a good grasp of technique, but our writing tends to be formulaic and rules-driven. Rules-driven writing gets you a passing grade, maybe higher, but it doesn't bring in the top marks. If you're always getting a B+, or getting lukewarm feedback from your advisors when you want to get glowing praise, you are stuck at competent performer level.

To get to expert performer level – and the excellent grades – you must work on developing your academic style, but that style must always be tempered by the discipline in which you are located. Every academic discipline can be considered a different kind of 'dialect' of academic English. To master the right dialect, you need to pay close attention to how and why it is produced. A writer stuck at the level of competent performer may not be attentive enough to the nuanced differences between different academic dialects. The competent performer has learned to mimic the style of writers they are reading, but they don't know why the text looks the way it does. The examples and exercises in this book are designed to help you learn the right academic dialect for you, by supplying the tools that help you critically examine these texts and replicate the language patterns. Once you know the reasons why academic texts look the way they do, you have more power to engineer your writing.

It's a long and often tough road, as we well know, but you must believe you can learn this skill. With enough practice and the right kind of feedback, eventually, you will become expert. You may only wish to be expert enough to survive the degree you are currently enrolled in, and that's okay too – we hope this book will offer enough strategies to get you there.

Crafting this book

All three of us are experienced writing teachers.

Inger has been working with research students for over 12 years. From her first degree as an architect to her PhD in hand gestures, Inger has always had a keen interest in communication. Her interest in academic writing style comes from an experience of teaching herself how to 'write academic' while trying to complete a Master's degree. Although she was considered more than competent at writing in high school, her experience of trying to please academics was bewildering. Through dogged persistence (and spending a lot of money on 'how to write' books), Inger eventually honed her academic writing skills and started to explore blogging, where she found her real writing passion. Because of her design background, Inger's approach to writing teaching is 'non-standard'; informed more from books and failure than from formal learning. When Open University Press offered Inger a chance to write a book on writing, she jumped at the chance to do one informed by all this failure to understand the 'hidden rules' of academic writing and written from a place of real empathy for the frustration many beginning academic writers feel. Inger invited Katherine and Shaun along on the ride because she didn't trust herself to write a whole book on such a difficult topic by herself. Lucky she did because she learned a heck of a lot more about writing from Katherine and Shaun!

Katherine has been helping postgraduate students with research and writing skills for over a decade. Most of the time she is a 'naturally' good writer, so she was amazed to find not everyone just 'got it', and started on a quest to reverse-engineer the pleasure, joy and confidence she felt whenever she had the chance to put words on paper. Katherine was lucky enough to go to Cambridge University to read English Literature, where learning to write, learning to read, and learning to construct an argument were the explicit focus of her undergraduate degree. A sometimes professional, occasionally award-winning side-line as a creative writer also gave her experience of working on writing, and explaining how to make writing better. Her research for her Honours, Master's, PhD and ever since, has been about how poets make their texts – their drafts, their composition strategies, how they work with other artists, and how they work in collaboration with others. She is still fascinated by these questions, and working with Inger and Shaun has taught her how much more there is still to explore.

Shaun has been teaching for over ten years across a number of disciplines. He is a qualified teacher of English as a second/other language, and has taught a wide variety of students ranging from casual learners of 'travel English' to academics wishing to better communicate their research. He also has extensive experience writing and delivering university pathway courses that focus on building academic skills and literacies. In his view, all university students are scholars in the true sense of that word, and he enjoys helping them realise this. Shaun's own research background is in the intersecting space between human genetics and anthropology – interdisciplinary research and the challenges it presents are one of his primary passions in scholarship. Writing did not come naturally to Shaun as an undergraduate student, so his goal in working with the writing of this book was to produce the kind of help manual that he wished he had had as a student.

Writing this book from multiple perspectives was a great strength, but also presented many challenges in composition. We came up with the recipe book idea early in the process, and it enabled us to break the writing into chunks that could be shared out between us. Two of us are enthusiastic bloggers, and we find the short writing format comfortable. We took the opportunity to test out the content on the Thesis Whisperer, which at the time of writing had a follower base of around 100,000 people. By exposing our 'messy' writing in public before committing it to the book, we got a sense of what was working and where we needed more clarification. After we had all finished our first draft of each chunk of writing, we uploaded our drafts to a shared Dropbox folder and proceeded to edit each other's work.

While we found ourselves in furious agreement most of the time – and personally learned a lot from reading each other's work – occasionally we found we had different approaches to some of the writing troubles we were trying to identify and solve. Rather than smooth these differences over, we decided to celebrate the diversity of opinions – but this presented us with a writing challenge of how to manage multiple voices. So, in this book, most of the time we use the royal 'we' and speak as one voice. Sometimes, when we want to highlight a difference of opinion or talk about ourselves, we speak in the third person, using that author's name. This means you will sometimes see sentences like 'Katherine likes to show her students . . .', 'Shaun recommends using . . .' or 'when Inger faces this problem, she . . .'. We hope this way of presenting highlights our productive differences and enables us to share many facets of our collective wisdom.

We all currently work in Australian universities, but we expect this book will be read around the world. There is a lot of variation in what people call those who study for research degrees, the people who help them, and the thing they write. We have chosen to use the word 'student' for people who are working towards PhDs, which may also make the book relevant to people undertaking Master's and Honours dissertations. The people likely to read your academic writing are described as your advisor (supervisor, professor, lecturer), examiners (in the US, this is your committee) and academic readers (peer reviewers, journal editors, anyone who picks up your work to cite for their own research). We have also used the word 'dissertation' to mean the document you write, and 'thesis' to mean your argument or hypothesis.

How to use this book

This book can be used two ways. While we imagine most of our readers are students or research degree students, we hope this book is useful for those tasked with marking coursework student essays or helping to shape doctoral dissertations.

Students can read the feedback they are getting from their advisors, and look up the relevant section. Each chapter addresses a big, common group of issues. Often you will need a few individual sections to address a complex academic writing trouble. Each section has a clear and accessible explanation of an issue, and then an example or exercise that you can do to see the solution in practice. You can then see how to write 'more critically', or make your argument 'flow'. Different chapters are likely to be more relevant at different stages of writing, so we expect you to dip in and out of the book as you write your dissertation.

Advisors can use this book to help them give better advice to students. This book documents more elaborate explanations of the writing problems that many advisors can offer. Teaching each student why a common problem is happening and how to fix it becomes very tedious over time. Or an advisor might be facing an issue for the first time, for example, due to cross-disciplinary research.

This book is like a diagnostic manual you might find in a doctor's surgery – listing common complaints and offering some 'treatments'. For that reason, we have kept the individual sections short. We imagine an advisor photocopying a couple of pages to give back with a manuscript edit to help the novice writer fix a recurring issue. We certainly intend to use the book this way ourselves.

1.2 Time management for academic writing: the Pomodoro Technique, Shut Up and Write, and boot camps

Some of the hardest things about academic writing are finding the time to do it, being efficient when you are doing it, and getting it done by the deadline. In this section, we will share the techniques we have found useful for all our academic writing projects – especially this book! We recommend you should be critical of any writing advice which suggests there is only one 'true way' to be a productive writer. We do not believe in 'binge' or 'snack' writing language, or the 'write or die' apps that proliferate on the web. We recommend you ignore any person, website or book that makes you feel bad about how many words you are producing per hour. All writing is good writing.

We have found the most useful academic writing advice suggests a mix between short, frequent writing blocks (at least weekly, but might be daily) and occasional writing intensives. Different kinds of writing are useful in different situations. We believe in external motivations for writing. Working with other people, a kitchen timer, or a massive deadline can be healthy and helpful ways to motivate you to write and write well (the massive deadline certainly helped get this book done!). A productive writing practice uses any and every useful technique – adapted to your circumstances and preferences. Here are some of our personal favourites.

The Pomodoro Technique

Francisco Cirillo developed a time-boxing system called the Pomodoro Technique in the 1980s. It's an incredibly simple and effective method to increase your writing productivity. The technique is named after Cirillo's tomato-shaped kitchen timer, which he used to do timed bursts of writing. The technique works on the basis that you lose concentration if you work for a long time without a break, and that you work well if you have a deadline coming up. The Pomodoro Technique is a way to break up your work into lots of small chunks with regular breaks, which helps you to work for longer and be more focused. You can use a kitchen timer, or a range of apps on your phone and computer – anything that will interrupt you after a certain length of time.

1 Choose what you are going to work on for your burst. Make it something you can achieve in your time box ('write three final paragraphs and the conclusion' works better than 'finish that essay').
2 Set your timer. The original Pomodoro Technique recommends a 25-minute period of uninterrupted work, but some people find 10 minutes or 90 minutes is more effective. Do what works for you!
3 Work on your task while the timer ticks down. If you are tempted to do something else, remember a break is coming up. Keep working. The discipline required is a bit like swimming a length of the pool – tell yourself you can't stop until you reach the end.
4 When the timer goes off, take a short break. We recommend about 1/5 of the work time as a sensible break (so, 5 minutes for a standard 25-minutes of working). Set your timer for the break. Stretch. Grab a glass of water. Deal with that urgent phone call. Look at your email.
5 When the timer goes off, get back into your task again.
6 Repeat four times before taking a more extended break, say, for lunch or dinner.
7 Alternatively, use the Pomodoro Technique to get a small task done during a tiny gap in your schedule.

The Pomodoro Technique is a wonderful way to increase your attention span and ability to focus on task. (Inger took about eight years of continuous practice to be able to concentrate on a single task for an hour or more without needing the clock.) It also helps avoid fatigue from focusing for too long without looking after yourself. (Katherine took about seven years to stop needing the clock to remind her to stretch and drink more water every 90 minutes.)

Shut Up and Write

The concept of Shut Up and Write is simple: meet up with others, and write. Typically, Shut Up and Write groups meet once a week in a café for one to two hours to write together and share conversation. Shut Up and Write groups use the Pomodoro Technique in a communal setting; using the breaks between stretches of work to socialise and grab a coffee: turning a writing group into a social support mechanism. Some people have a 'sit down and write' group, which is just as good and might be less challenging language for some people.

The Shut Up and Write concept originated in the San Francisco Bay Area, among creative writers, but, thanks to social media, has spread among research students around the world. Inger was one of the original advocates for the 'Shut Up and Write' movement among academics and helped it to become a global movement by writing about it on the Thesis Whisperer blog. The idea behind the concept is to make the act of writing fun and relaxing, as the San Francisco group puts it: 'No critiquing, exercises, lectures, ego, competition or feeling guilty.'

Exercise

Anyone can start a Shut Up and Write group – you don't need permission or any extra resources, but we have found it works best if you do the following:

- Meet at a regular, pre-arranged time and place.
- Create a contact point for new members, using social media is a great idea.
- Keep the writing sprints – or 'Pomodoros' – short. Between the Pomodoros, take as much time as the group would like to drink hot beverages, talk and eat. Have one person willing to act as 'Pomodoro chief' to make everyone get back to work again within a reasonable time.
- Work on anything, so long as it's work – transcription, analysis, reading, organising your notes. No exercises or judgement remember? The only rule is to be silent during the Pomodoros.
- Accept that Shut Up and Write is not for everyone. Some people may only come once; others will be regulars.

Katherine did about 90 per cent of her writing for this book in her weekly Shut Up and Write group. Even if she didn't work on the book at any other time, it got bumped forward regularly because of two focused hours on a Thursday morning. Shut Up and Write can be adapted for whole-day write-ups, small student-led sessions, or daily writing.

Thesis Boot Camp and writing retreats

While regular writing practices – daily writing with the Pomodoro Technique or joining a Shut Up and Write group – help you move your research along, you may sometimes benefit from a writing retreat. A writing retreat is any longer period where you can focus exclusively on writing, preferably in a new location (some people call this a 'writing binge', but we don't like that negative language). Many people find a long weekend is hugely productive. Katherine's preferred writing retreat is three days completely alone. On the other hand, a writing retreat with other people can be hugely beneficial to both your motivation and productivity. Inger takes a group of friends down to the beach once a year and likes to compare these writing retreats to exercise classes: there's nothing like a big group of people around you, typing furiously, to stop you from slacking off! Everyone can benefit from an annual or quarterly writing retreat. Your university may run one, or you might get together with a few friends and hire a cottage in the country.

One of the most successful versions of the academic writing retreat model is a 'Thesis Boot Camp' – three intensive days of writing for late-stage PhD students. Some people think Thesis Boot Camp means locking unprepared people in a room and shouting at them to keep writing, but a well-run Thesis Boot Camp, supervised by experienced personnel, is a well-researched, encouraging and productive environment that can transform your relationship to your writing. Similar to Shut Up and Write, the mean-sounding title and promise of unfettered productivity are a big attraction to weary PhD students who want to get that dissertation out of their life!

Dr Peta Freestone was the original designer of the award-winning Thesis Boot Camp programme. Peta ran the programme initially at the University of Melbourne in 2012 and further developed the concept in collaboration with Dr Katherine Firth and Dr Liam Connell. The Thesis Boot Camp (TBC) concept has proved a powerful formula for research higher degree students around the world. Since 2014, the original TBC team have been working in partnership with other universities to introduce the programme to new cohorts. Katherine still regularly helps run boot camps at the University of Melbourne. Liam regularly runs boot camps around Australia, and Peta runs them worldwide, and they will train people at other universities to run their own. Inger was one of Liam's trainees and now runs four Thesis Boot Camps a year at ANU. We have noticed that people around the world have been calling their writing retreats 'Thesis Boot Camp', but most of these are nothing like the original programme Peta designed.[1]

Peta, Liam and Katherine's programme is carefully structured, based on extensive research on factors leading to successful writing. TBC is designed and developed specifically for late stage students who have read, thought and processed so much, for years, before they attend a Thesis Boot Camp. They are expected to have researched and planned the chapter before they come. Participants are set a 'stretch target' of 20,000 words in two and a half days. At the TBC Inger runs at ANU, everyone writes at least 5000 words, but most participants will write between 5000 and 15,000; two or three people reach the 20,000-word target. This much intensive writing is not something you should be aiming to achieve at home on a regular basis. TBC is designed to be a one-off writing extravaganza when you are close to completion. Writing so many words early in a PhD candidature would not be very easy – or useful.

All good Thesis Boot Camps have extensive pre-camp training and exercises to support students to arrive prepared. Any writing retreat needs to be part of a broader training and support environment, including support from other service areas of your university, such as the library or academic skills unit.

Thesis Boot Camps create communities, and that is a beautiful thing that can be leveraged for more writing success! In some places, including the University of Melbourne and ANU, participants who have completed TBC are eligible to take part in 'veterans' days' or other writing communities to support ongoing writing. The ANU TBC is hugely popular and always has a very long waiting list, but the value is more profound than its popularity. Inger's research into the outcomes of participants in TBC has shown the programme significantly reduces attrition among PhD students. Inger's research results suggest it is the community aspect of the TBC experience that is most powerful and long-lasting.

Time to edit, read more, rewrite

As the rest of this book will show, the work of getting words onto the page is but the first step. You will need multiple rounds of editing before the words are scholarly. Nearly everyone fails to leave enough time to edit – including us! The last stages of this book were down to the wire. Inger got a lot of her editing done at a Thesis Boot Camp; Katherine got most her editing done on holiday in Italy. Both regular small editing sessions and long editing retreats are likely to be necessary for the final stage of any writing project. Schedule enough time in before your deadline – especially if you are like us and spend more of your time bashing out a blog-post or making comments on other people's work, than producing highly polished text. Editing is time-consuming even when you know what needs to be done and have the tools to do it well!

Where next?

Now you have the foundations of what this book is for. You know how you might fit the advice we give you into the bigger picture of writing, getting feedback, and revising your academic writing. You have some strategies for finding the time to do the work. From here, you might want to read through the whole book, or you might want to jump straight to the chapter that looks most relevant to you. We've tried to make the headings useful, but we also have an index. Whichever way you read from here, we hope you find this a practical guide that helps you fix your academic writing trouble, and succeed in your studies.

2 'Your writing doesn't sound very academic': how to convince your reader you belong

In this chapter, we help you understand, and replicate, appropriate 'academic tone'. We show you how to be 'argumentative' (without getting into an argument). We guide you on the right ways to signal you 'belong', through use of verbs, references, and footnotes. We aim to help you become fluent and confident in 'Academicese', while recognising there are some issues with the way that Academicese looks to outsiders, and how hard it is to write.

Getting Academicese wrong can be catastrophic. Consider this real feedback given to a PhD student from a humanities discipline just one day before they submitted their thesis:

> This dissertation is a train wreck. You have no rationale and it appears to have been written by a four-year-old. There is no critical evaluation or analysis in this anywhere. You can be very glad I am not your examiner. I will sign off and let you submit but it is at your own risk. You've greatly disappointed me.[2]

What could have prompted this attack? Aside from being unhelpful (and delivered far too late for the student to do anything about it), the statement 'There is no critical evaluation or analysis in this anywhere' lacks context. What, specifically, went wrong here? We show students who get (hopefully less extreme) versions of this feedback how to fix their writing and sound like academics.

Skilful use of Academicese is needed to take a position, claim a genealogy, show you are smart, gather your posse, defend against attacks, and make points of your own. If this sounds a bit like something out of Machiavelli's *The Prince*, that's because it is. The norms of university life and writing are influenced by its medieval history. We explain why the invasion of England by the Normans in 1066 influences what vocabulary sounds 'smart'. We show you how the early modern practices of 'Oxbridge' college life are the reason that fencing is the best metaphor to describe how to make written arguments. We explore the deep connections of power and knowledge that make references into magical talismans that protect you from the curse of the nit-picky examiner. We even show you how knowing which verb to use – and when – can give you a seat at the High Table (or the modern equivalent, the middle-class academic dinner party).

If you think what happened 800 years ago is irrelevant to now, that's because 'privilege' tends to be invisible. We believe in making the operations of privilege transparent, so everyone can have an equal chance of success.

Becoming an academic researcher is a journey from being an apprentice to being part of a global community of experts in your field. These communities are created and sustained through what Becher and Trowler (2001) called 'academic tribes', built within faculties, through key journals and conferences and conversations among peers. Academicese is fundamental to this process. All academic writers use a dialect of Academicese which allows them to signal membership of their academic 'thought tribe'. The job of the novice research writer is to produce text that shows they are ready to join the conversation as a peer (including peer reviewing other experts' work).

You might be the first person in your family to try to get a PhD (as Katherine was) or even the first in your family to go to university (as Inger was). You might have come from a very different education system and need to learn the new rules. We have found that it is usually outsiders who need someone to explain the tacit rules that everyone else seems to naturally 'just get'. People who 'just get' these rules therefore find it hard to explain how and why the rules work to outsiders: that is the key reason for the frustratingly obscure feedback we have observed on so many dissertation and essay drafts. If your reader can't articulate what is wrong, you cannot fix your academic writing trouble. We believe that anyone can learn the rules of Academicese and that making these unspoken rules explicit means great researchers can successfully write about the incredible research they are doing to improve the world, regardless of whether they learned Latin or fencing at school.

2.1 How to unlearn high school English

Our high school English teachers do essential work. The training they provide on reading between the lines and identifying a writer's intention makes a valuable contribution to the academic skill set of students who enter university. There can be no doubt that the sorts of writing tasks undertaken for English or English Literature classes offer solid opportunities to improve your ability to put together arguments and convey your thoughts, but they can also be a source of writing patterns and preferences that do not always translate well into the university environment. Continuing to use this 'high school' style of writing can result in negative feedback on structure, and argumentation.

This section gives some examples of writing conventions that students learn in their high school classes, and how they differ from what is expected in writing at a university level. We offer these insights to help you self-diagnose what Shaun calls 'fossilised habits', and update your writing strategies.

The traditional essay style vs journal publication style

The writing English teachers encourage in high school is process-oriented, by which we mean it is intended to be read for evidence that the writer can write, not for content. The essay genre favoured by English teachers is what we call the 'traditional essay', which is a different beast from the academic paper or dissertation. By 'traditional essay', we mean an essay that moves through an argument fluidly, with an emphasis on paragraph linking to guide the reader, as opposed to subheadings. The traditional essay is intended to be read in-depth and appreciated as a literary art form. The order of the points structures the traditional essay – particularly the dreaded 'five-paragraph essay' format: the introduction is the introduction because it is the first paragraph, and further points are introduced with loose paragraph linking. There is an emphasis on presenting both sides of an argument and only coming to the writer's position, or 'stance', in the conclusion paragraph.

In a university setting, advisors and examiners want an explicit argument, signposted as early as possible. This style of writing is in keeping with what most academics are used to reading. Journal articles and conference papers are generally written as clearly as possible to tight word limits. Rather than assuming the argument can emerge through paragraph order, the argument should be presented clearly, so that it can be identified and evaluated by a reader applying minimal cognitive effort. Thus, clear topic sentences are critical, and linking between paragraphs should be done with precision (see Chapter 3 for more advice on this).

Signposting the argument

While it is far from universal, students in secondary school are often encouraged to avoid direct 'signposting' language like 'this essay will argue . . .'. By contrast, direct argument statements are generally welcome in university-level writing. Your academic reader wants to know what you are trying to argue right up front and is not willing to figure this out for themselves. As one of Inger's PhD advisors was fond of saying: 'Academic writing is not a murder mystery, we know who died in the first paragraph.' The crisp style favoured by most academics means trying to avoid using signposting language may leave your academic reader dangerously confused. In addition to a clear and direct argument statement, the reader also wants an unambiguous overview of what your essay (or chapter if you are writing a dissertation) will cover and in what order. Again, a direct statement like 'this will be done by first x, then y, and finally z' is both easy to write, and understand. Most academic writing is not very elegant, but it gets the job done. As Paul Silva put it: 'Novelists and poets are the landscape artists and portrait painters; academics are the people with big paint sprayers who repaint your basement' (2007, p. 45).

The structure of a given piece of writing is more visible when you use subheadings. Subheadings are even more important when your work is under assessment. Mullins and Kiley (2010) researched how academic examiners approach the task of assessing a dissertation and found many do not read a dissertation in the order the writer intended. Subheadings take on increased importance in this examination context. However, while the use of subheadings in university-level writing is widespread, it differs between disciplines.

We recommend that for any given writing task, you should ask your advisor whether the use of subheadings is acceptable – or look at successful examples, such as previously published dissertations in the discipline.

When writing your subheadings, be sure to use language that links clearly to your argument statement and overview in your introduction. Remember, the objective in using subheadings is to reduce the amount of hard work that your reader needs to do when they skim read your work. They also serve as useful 'anchor points' for people to return to a section for further information or to re-read the content.

Language style

Traditional essays are not mere tools for the conveying of information; they are intended to be appreciated aesthetically. In traditional essays, a certain elegance of expression will get you a good grade. Literary essays like Thoreau's 'Civil Disobedience' or Camus' 'The Myth of Sisyphus' are appreciated for the sophistication of their prose as well as their message. In contrast, most contemporary academic readers judge the worth of your writing by the argument, and the reasons and evidence you deploy to convince them of it. In other words, elegance is secondary to the clarity of your message.

If you are a person who appreciates reading and writing for enjoyment and loved high school English class, it can be a little disheartening to hear that most academic writing is boringly mechanical. Just try to keep in mind that when you are writing an essay or a thesis, you are not writing for yourself. Your audience is often pressed for time; they want to be convinced of something, not entertained. Just try to spray-paint the basement with minimal fuss, as tidily and quickly as you can. If you follow our advice here, and in the rest of the book, your text will be easier to read and therefore likely to be perceived as lucid and organised; in short, more scholarly.

Exercises to improve academic writing

You can increase the clarity and ease of reading of your work by following these rules of thumb:

1 If a sentence is longer than 2.5 lines, you should consider breaking it up (see Section 4.2 on sentences).
2 Try to limit a single sentence to a single idea (see Chapter 4).
3 Adverbs like 'clearly', 'surprisingly', 'obviously' can often be removed without changing the meaning of your work (see Section 5.6 on filler words).
4 Avoid disrupting your sentences with what Shaun calls 'island clauses', lengthy parenthetical comments (see Section 5.4 on hypotaxis and parataxis).
5 Be sure that your paragraphs and sections have distinct themes and do not bleed into one another. (For further information on themes, see Section 4.4 on themes and rhemes in sentences.)

2.2 'This sounds chatty or not scholarly': getting the academic tone right

Being told that your work 'doesn't sound academic' or 'sounds like spoken language' is extremely common, and yet it can be difficult to act on this feedback. Even academics who recognise 'academic tone' when they see it, can find it hard to put their finger on exactly which language features are responsible for making something sound 'not academic'. The truth is that most academics learn how to produce academic tone through a process of osmosis. Over years of reading academic text, they learn to intuitively pick up on the language patterns that are common to scholarly publications.

Luckily, the linguistic underpinnings of 'sounding academic' are readily understandable. Here we will show you one way to quickly and easily gain that seemingly elusive academic tone.

Before getting onto what academic tone is, we think it is important to talk about what it is not. It is common for students to think that sounding academic is about complexity, their first impression of academic English as a genre is that it's full of overly long and 'waffly' sentences. However, if you try to 'sound academic' by mimicking this style, you will be (rightly) criticised for not being sufficiently concise. (See Chapter 5 on dealing with 'waffle'.) More important is knowing which words to choose, through knowing how the word came into English.

A brief history lesson is in order. Following the withdrawal of the Romans from Britain in the fifth century CE, much of what is now England was invaded and subsequently occupied by various groups from the coasts of Europe. Most notable among these were the Angles and Saxons (the term 'England' actually derives from the name of the first of these three groups, and the basis of the term 'Anglo-Saxon'). These were Germanic-speaking peoples who brought language forms and customs that would form the core of our modern English language. Under their rule, the dominant language of England was Old-English or Old-Saxon; the language of the famous poem *Beowulf*.

In 1066, William the Conqueror and his Norman French-speaking compatriots invaded England. Under his rule, and that of his descendants, the language of all things official in England came to be French. At the same time, like much of the rest of Europe, the language of scholarship, the law and the church remained Latin. Thus, many French and Latin words were absorbed into English. What's more, these words tended to be used by people when they wanted to be 'official'; if you wanted to be understood by your French-speaking overlords, you needed to use words that they would understand!

The effect on English has been long-lasting. Writing in 'plain English' can sound more informal, because Anglo-Saxon/Germanic terms are those used by the conquered peasants, not by judges, scholars and kings. To this day, when we want to sound academic, official, 'fancy' or high-brow, we tend to choose words derived from French and Latin ('Latinate').

Here's an example, which sounds 'informal', until we replace the Germanic word with a Latinate one:

> The folk in the study were given forms to fill in. We then asked them to think about the questions they were shown. (Informal – Germanic)
> The participants in the study were provided with forms to complete. We then requested that they consider the questions they were shown. (Academic – Latinate)

The two sentences are equivalent in meaning, but the second achieves the aim of sounding pleasing to our imaginary Norman lords, using more formal language. A tiny change in choosing a word with a different origin, but sufficient for the second example to sound quite a lot more 'academic' than the first. You will notice that the Latinate terms are also more precise, Germanic terms tend to be more general.

So how can you know which words originate in which language? A good dictionary can help as they usually also have an entry with the word's etymology (the technical word for its origin). If you ask Google to define 'participants', for example, you get a clear 'family tree' diagram with the word origin. If you find that your word of choice has a Germanic origin, use a thesaurus to find an alternative and then check its origin. Within a few minutes, you can usually find a Latinate alternative.

Before you get too carried away with Latinising your work, it's important to point out that you shouldn't overdo it. Think of this process as being like adding salt to soup: a little bit makes the soup taste better, but too much can ruin it.

Table 2.1   Shaun's table of examples for choosing Latinate or Germanic academic terms

Kind of term	Germanic terms	Latinate terms
Adjective (describing word)	Big	Large, significant, extensive
	Good	Valuable, advantageous, appropriate, approved
	Main	Principal, significant, primary, essential, fundamental
Phrasal verb (action words that have more than one word)	Fill in	Complete, substitute
	Think about	Consider, examine, appraise, review
Adverb	Fast	Rapid, prompt, sudden
	Strongly	Powerfully, forcefully, intensely

Changing too many words can leave your work sounding pompous. A good way to find the right balance of word origins is to examine the word choices used by good authors in your field (see Table 2.1). For more examples, see our section on verbs in Chapter 2.

2.3 'Who are you standing with?': being argumentative in your writing

Do you ever get accused of not being 'present' in your writing? We are thinking of feedback like 'I can't hear your voice', 'what do YOU think?' or 'not argumentative enough!'. It is not sufficient to just discuss the facts and put forward the evidence in academic writing; you need to convince the reader of the claims you make through argumentation. Sometimes this arguing involves admitting the limits of your arguments, recognising the culture around you, and accepting your position in a hierarchy that not many people will admit to existing. Confused yet? Read on!

Writing 'like an academic' (speaking 'Academicese') involves demonstrating your authority to know. You demonstrate your position, and your right to have a position, through a range of strategies including argumentation, theory, methods, citations, and jargon. To make matters more complicated, as a student you must take up the position of junior expert – contributing to your field as a newcomer, while not coming across as an upstart. How to set out an argument is explored extensively in Chapters 3 and 6. Here we are more concerned with explaining how Academicese contains built-in ways of demonstrating your authority and position.

Fencing is an excellent metaphor for arguing in Academicese. Fencing is a highly codified and safe form of combat with medieval courtly antecedents; still practised globally at an elite level. Like academic argument, fencing has attacking and defensive moves: both are assertive rather than all-out aggressive, and many unfair attacking moves are considered inappropriate and out of bounds. Like academic writing, when it works, fencing is all about the elaborate exchange of momentum. Each block and step backwards is not a loss of progress, but a chance to reset your posture to enable the next attack to be more effective. Moreover, both fencing and academic argumentation are highly technical and precise. Sloppily waving your sword around may work in a mud-spattered mêlée, but duelling with swords is a gentleman's way of solving a disagreement. This analogy works well if you swap it over to magic duels with spells and wands, as in *Harry Potter*. In fiction, the connection between knowledge and power is something wizards must learn to control and wield (we like the idea of becoming academic wizards). Our examples – fencing and wizardry – seem charmingly archaic, but that's because universities have been in existence for over 800 years.

There are many fossilised remnants of medieval practices that apply to academic writing. Scholastic (late medieval) university teaching and learning were characterised by a range of interactive techniques, including diagrams, wall-charts, debates, and copious marginalia and annotations. Take as just one example the *lectio* (or lecture, though the word also means 'reading'), when students had to listen and stay silent while their teacher read (or sometimes riffed on) a prescribed text. The *lectio* was followed by the *meditatio* (or meditation) when students sat in silence and reflected on what they had heard. Silent reflection was followed by *quaestiones* (or questions) – a time for students to ask questions of the lecturer. Sometimes difficult questions could be covered in daily *disputationes* (or debates) either between senior experts in the field or between students.

All these academic moves (listening, thinking, questioning and arguing) are embedded in the norms of academic writing, and in critical thinking more generally. You are expected to take in the ideas of experts by reading and thinking about them. You should then develop good questions and use these to take up your own position in the broader debates of your field. You are a student debating a senior expert in the field, so your teacher/examiner is judging who wins the debate. The *viva voce* doctoral examination (or oral defence) is another remaining example of this practice. They will also be judging your 'moves': do you manage all those power relations with grace, and still win with panache?

As you move from writing literature reviews and research essays in your undergraduate degree, you must start establishing your own voice and position. To do this, you need to stop relying entirely on the works of other scholars and bring your own thoughts and ideas to the table as well. By about six months into a full-time research degree project, you should know a bit more than your advisors about your specific area. From this point on, especially as the gap between your knowledge and theirs grows, you will be expected to stop always deferring to their knowledge and start leading the discussion. Your advisors are still very useful as a broader expert in the field and as an experienced writer and researcher, but you are the one making the original contributions to knowledge. Summon up your courage, clutch your wand or sword, and start using your writing to teach others what you know.

Academic writing isn't quite like other kinds of writing. The academy is both a community (we have norms, we have in-language, we have rules) and a collection of experts (we have technical language and structures that we share). Demonstrating your power and provenance requires using the in-language and rules to demonstrate your expertise.

If you are third-generation, university-educated, or went to that kind of high school, or had great Honours or Master's degree advisors, these norms might feel natural to you. You may have absorbed the right ways to write through reading journal articles, other theses, and taking on feedback from your undergraduate essays. This feeling for the right way to do things is what Barbara Lovitts (2007) calls the 'implicit' aspects of higher education, and others have called the 'hidden curriculum'.

Whether you are writing by feel or by learned rules, you must use four main techniques: citations, theory, methods and jargon.

Citations

Experienced academics use citations strategically to shore up their claims to knowledge. As Bruno Latour put it: 'A paper that does not have references is like a child without an escort walking in the night in a big city it does not know: isolated, lost, anything may happen to it' (1993, p. 33). We discuss using citations in much more detail later in this chapter in Section 2.6 How to use references to show who your academic network is (and isn't) and Section 2.7 Using references as magic tokens to power up your writing.

Theory

Theories are excellent for giving you a lens to look at a problem, dataset or case study, but they are not just ideas, they are philosophies. Embedded in every theory is already a highly specific and nuanced argument and position, which varies in every discipline and area. To further complicate matters, the word 'theory' can mean different things in different academic contexts (we do a deep dive into the ins and outs of using theory in 'Theory wars' in Section 2.4, and look at interdisciplinary ways of knowing in Chapter 3).

Method

As you probably know, but it's worth repeating, choose your methods carefully. Different disciplines have different norms: the 'right' method may mean quantitative rather than qualitative research, or it may mean double-blind, placebo-controlled studies. Some fields are conservative (like Classical studies) and prefer you to demonstrate that you still use the old methods of historicism and exegetical readings. Some fields subscribe to a 'fast fashion' mentality: methods go out of fashion quickly. Sometimes you must show you are at the forefront of a research field by using the newest methodology, perhaps using cutting-edge technology like MRI machines, big data, digital humanities, or mixed methods. We are striving to keep things as non-disciplinary as possible in this book and won't be saying anything more about methods; consult your advisor and survey articles published in the top journals in your field to ensure your methods are right.

Jargon

Jargon can be exclusionary, or clunky, or showing off, but it can also be useful. Frequently, jargon is a shortened form of expert language that you can expect your reader to understand. Using jargon makes things faster for everyone. For example, Katherine can use the term 'iambic pentameter' in order to avoid saying 'a line of poetry with ten alternating stressed and unstressed syllables starting on an unstressed syllable' (that's 16 words instead of two).

However, do your homework and avoid using jargon words incorrectly. Katherine is enraged by people misusing 'neoliberal' and Inger develops an eye twitch whenever someone brings up 'the meritocracy'. Incorrect usage betrays the amateur.

So, *en garde*, fellow writer! Take up your *epée*, adopt a fighting pose, let us salute each other. Let us fight, and may the best argument win!

2.4 Getting beyond 'descriptive' writing by entering the theory wars

Sometimes we see feedback on student drafts like: 'merely descriptive', 'this is not a model', 'add more theory', or even an existential 'WHY???'. This kind of feedback indicates you are failing to provide enough – or the right kind of – theorising text. In the previous section, we pointed out that deploying theory was one of the ways that you construct your authority as an academic writer. However, a dissertation is not like a petrol tank; you can't just 'top it up' with some missing theory ingredient and drive off into the sunset. So, what can you do?

First – and most importantly – relax. Exactly what constitutes 'theory', and how to do it properly, are tricky; even experienced academics struggle. Part of the problem is that the word 'theory' is used as a catch-all phrase for the important explanatory work – the 'why is it so?' dimension of the research. Like everything in academia, discipline matters. Kiley (2009) points out that the word 'theory' is used differently by scientists and humanities scholars, with the former often using the word 'model' instead. Academics know most students struggle with theory. Usually, in postgraduate work, your advisor's role is to be a sounding board: a person who listens and helps you develop theoretical ideas or models, rather than someone who 'corrects' you. This might be a more equal teaching and learning relationship than you, or your advisor, is used to, which might be why we often encounter students and advisors in serious conflict over theory. Students report being frustrated by their advisor's endless questions and lack of concrete suggestions; advisors complain that a student 'just doesn't get it' or 'can't think for themselves' (a serious accusation in academic-land). Theory conflict is fertile ground for people to start making unfair assumptions: academics can assume students are lazy, or intellectually not up to the task, while students point the finger at academics for being disengaged or uncaring.

So, let's take a step back and think about what theory is for a moment. Sutton and Shaw (1995) usefully point out what theory is not: theory is not citations or references to other people who have theories; it is not a hypothesis, where you state what you think the outcome might be; nor is theory data where you describe or represent the situation. Theory is the 'why' of research and what theory you use, or subscribe to, should affect how you write. Let's explore some examples in practice.

Humanities and Social Sciences (HASS) and creative disciplines

In HASS and creative disciplines, we often invoke the theory by talking about the theorist. For example, if you set out to read Jane Austen's *Mansfield Park* through Judith Butler's *Gender Trouble*, you start with a view of gender as performative. You then focus on gender in the text, perhaps exploring the ways the characters behave to reinforce or disturb the gender norms. A theory thus situates and establishes an argument, simply by being used. An excellent method of constructing an original contribution to knowledge in the humanities, arts and social sciences is to bring a new theory to a well-known set of information. HASS and creative disciplines do not often agree on what constitutes knowledge and truth: students must navigate their way through a landscape of competing theories. Their literature reviews usually attempt to be inclusive of multiple approaches, even if they select one lens for their research.

Science, technology, engineering and maths (STEM)

Theories in science and technology tend to be framed as an idea about how things work. Good examples are the theory of relativity, string theory, theory of evolution, or germ theory. Some STEM research looks at raw data and tries to find an explanation for it, but more often a scientist takes a general theory and explores it using new data. For example, if we have a theory about how mechanoreceptors build our sense of touch in the brain, can we then predict how we will respond to certain types of objects touching skin? Your theory will affect what you look at and how you interpret your findings. For example, if evolutionary theory informs your observations of animal behaviour, you will tend to see changes as adaptations. Since theory and interpretations are linked, it is vital that scientists stay up to date with current theories. If your theory of how a disease spreads is based on old-fashioned ideas of miasma, you won't be looking at water sources for bacteria and will miss the culprit entirely. For this reason, literature reviews in science list the most recent papers, rather than attempt a holistic view of the whole development of an area.

Theory and positioning yourself through text

Your approach to theory should have profound and subtle effects on your writing. You will note in our section on STEM, above, we talked about 'evolutionary theory' and not 'Darwinism'. In science, the focus tends to be more about the ideas than the person who came up with them. Reality is assumed to be separate from the person who is observing it, which affects the way that other people's ideas are 'imported' into your work. Hyland (2004) shows how writers in STEM disciplines tend to do more information-prominent citations. Here's a fictitious example:

> Children under the age of five dislike the sensation of herbaceous plants underfoot (Mewburn, 2009). The data in Table 1 (above) show that the most sensitive age (where children most dislike walking on grass) is 18 months, with greater acceptance from the age of 21 months onwards.

In the first sentence of our example, previous research findings are presented as fact and the information-prominent citation privileges the information over the person who made it. In the second sentence, the information is unproblematically used to build an extension to the theory about toddlers hating grass.

By contrast, writers in HASS disciplines would disagree about the fundamental claim unless they belonged to the same 'thought tribe'. This means that the sentences would be written differently, depending on how much the HASS researcher agreed with the theorist. The sentence construction emphasises the role of the theorist in the making of knowledge. Once the original author has been placed in the text, the HASS writer can position themselves (subtly) closer to, or further away from, the original author.

A HASS writer who was in sympathy with Mewburn might say:

> At the end of her small, participant observation study, Mewburn (2009) found that children under the age of five dislike the sensation of herbaceous plants underfoot, and *theorised* that all young children hate grass.

But if the HASS writer did not agree with Mewburn's methods, they might write:

> At the end of her participant observation study, Mewburn (2009) claimed that children under the age of five dislike the sensation of herbaceous plants underfoot, and then *assumes* that all young children hate grass.

Or, if the HASS writer wants to reject Mewburn's methods entirely, they might write:

> At the end of her small participant observation study, Mewburn (2009) made the *specious* claim that children under the age of five dislike the sensation of herbaceous plants underfoot, *making the unfounded assumption* that all young children hate grass.

Be careful how you approach the placement of citations. In STEM, writers focus more on the weight of ideas. The information-prominent citation style is a way of building authority through emphasising an object interest in 'the facts', and avoiding the appearance of entering into intellectual combat with the authors of the work. (You may be in combat, you just don't talk about it in scientific academic writing.) In HASS, supporting or rejecting a given author's ideas signals one's position in the discipline (in Section 2.5 on 'using verbs to signal you belong', we go into the use of verbs in more detail).

You will look like an amateur if you use mostly information-prominent citations when you should use an author-prominent style – and vice versa. The placing of references aligns with the way that different research disciplines like to approach theory building: generally, scientists seek to add a brick to the wall of existing ideas, while the HASS author seeks to renovate or rebuild it!

2.5 Using verbs to signal you belong: plus a verb cheat sheet

You might remember the crushing feedback we quoted in the introduction to this chapter, 'This dissertation is a train wreck. You have no rationale and it appears to have been written by a four-year-old. There is no critical evaluation or analysis in this anywhere.' If you get critical feedback like 'there is not evaluation or analysis', it may be something as small as they way you use verbs. This may seem trivial, but we will show that it is in fact fundamental to the way academic tribes make knowledge.

We have already pointed out that academics do not all write the same way. All academic writers are trying to persuade, but they are trying to persuade different audiences to accept different kinds of facts. These 'facts' are made by collectives of academics who use similar methods, with similar assumptions. We call these collectives 'academic disciplines' and give them different names: physics, economics, anthropology. Different language conventions develop in these discipline communities, just like languages do in a country or region. According to Becher and Trowler (2001), the language conventions of each 'academic tribe' are connected to the way each discipline makes knowledge. One place you can clearly see these differences in action is the way each academic tribe uses verbs.

Verbs are what your primary school teacher called 'doing words': words that express actions. The actions can be physical (run, jump, hop, skip), mental (thought, pondered, imagined), or a state of being (are, is, was, were, will be). What your teacher might not have told you is that verbs have complex functions in academic writing. One way to sound more forceful and 'academic' is to deploy the right kind of verbs properly. Verbs send subtle signals; forming a 'sub-text' in academic writing. If you get the verbs wrong, you don't sound very academic.

You can spot special academic verb work most clearly in sentences that deal with the literature. Sometimes, the absence of a verb is an important as its presence. As we highlighted in the previous section, when scientists are evaluating the work of other scientists, they favour what Hyland (2004) calls an 'information-prominent' citation style; the reference merely appears in brackets at the end of a statement. Here's a fictitious example:

> 'Wand weevils prefer to consume oak or bamboo wands' (Snape, 2010). When 50 wand weevils were placed on a wand made of holly, they did not attack the wood.

Here Snape's published research about oak and bamboo is used to lend support to the author's own research about holly. The writer could have also used an author-prominent style, like so:

> Snape (2010) demonstrated that wand weevils prefer to consume oak or bamboo wands.

The word 'demonstrated' is a reporting verb. According to Hyland, academics use three different types of reporting verbs to describe the work of others:

Research acts: verbs that refer to real-world activities, usually found in statements of findings (e.g. observe, discover, notice, show) or procedures (e.g. analyse, calculate, assay, explore).

Cognition acts: verbs that are concerned with mental processes (e.g. believe, conceptualise, suspect, view).

Discourse acts: verbs that recall different kinds of speech (e.g. ascribe, discuss, hypothesise, state).

(2004, p. 28)

Hyland goes on to describe how different disciplines have different verb preferences; the humanities tend to favour discourse act verbs (suggest, discuss), and the sciences tend to favour research act verbs (report, describe). Scientists tend be less interested in who did the work than in the work that was done, therefore the verbs are about actions (see Chapter 5 for how this also manifests in the use of the passive voice). In the Humanities, the person who did the work is important, so the verbs tend to reflect discourse acts – what the person said and how they said it. Over the last 30 years or so, the professions – nurses, architects, artists and others – have started to do PhDs and develop their new disciplinary ways of writing. In the professions, what counts as 'correct academic style' is still evolving; you should check what makes sense for your field.

Sometimes we see writers in the humanities using information-prominent citation style and leaving out the verbs on the mistaken assumption that it makes them sound more 'serious' and 'scholarly'. It does – but it makes them sound like a seriously scholarly scientist, not a serious historian. Likewise, a scientist who uses a verb like 'argues' instead of 'shows' is putting attention on the researcher, and failing to acknowledge the social convention in the sciences that who did the work is not important.

Academic authors in all disciplines use verbs to evaluate. They might imply you think the original author is telling the truth or not, for example:

Snape (2010) *established* that wand weevils prefer some woods over others. [claim is true]

Snape (2010) *exaggerated* the wand weevil preferences. [claim is not true]

It's rare that we are that certain about other people's research. It's far more likely you just want to say Snape did the work and not make a judgement one way or the other. Scientists tend to use verbs like 'show' a lot because they do not suggest much about the author of the work. For example:

Snape (2010) *showed* wand weevils' preference for oak and bamboo.

But how about if you are concerned that Snape has failed to take into account the socio-political context of weevil infestation? In this case, you want to do a gentle critique, without completely negating the original work. You could use a neutral verb that is just a little bit positive or negative (again drawing on Hyland 2004).

> Snape (2010) *argued* that wand weevils exist in greater numbers in the summer. [author positive]
>
> Snape (2010) *asserted* that wand weevils exist in greater numbers in the summer. [author critical]

While we say this is a more neutral verb, there is in fact a big difference between a scholar who 'argues' and one who merely 'asserts'. Look up both words in the dictionary and you will see what we mean. A scholar who argues typically has evidence and therefore is more scholarly than one who asserts. Neither sentence really indicates whether Snape is right or wrong in his assumptions about the seasonal behaviour of wand weevils, but they do act as a subtext to tell your reader what you think about Snape's work.

By using a verb to express your evaluation of someone else's work you avoid directly stating your opinion; your reader must 'read between the lines'. In this respect, academic writing is passive aggressive; academics routinely avoid saying directly what they mean.

In an academic paper, you would never, for example, write:

> Snape's (2010) *claim* about wand weevils is shit. Don't bother reading his work, it's rubbish.

As well as using the Germanic root word 'shit', the sentence is just not . . . polite. You might instead say:

> Snape (2010) *provided* insufficient evidence to *support* his *claims* about wood weevils.

This sentence means the same thing, but it's polite – at least according to dominant cultural norms in academia.

Academic politeness is not like ordinary politeness – it's very interested in status, in being combative, in scoring points. Like manners at the worst kind of middle-class dinner party, politeness is more about showing off your cultural capital than it is about sharing love and knowledge. Many Indigenous students, people who are the first in a family to go to university, and other 'academic outsiders', tend to recognise these passive aggressive politeness tactics for what they are straight away. When Inger shared this dinner party analogy with one Indigenous Wiradjuri woman, the student laughed and said: 'Right, so to succeed in the academy I have to write like an uptight white person? That makes perfect sense. I'm surrounded by them all the time.'[3] Unless you want to take the risk of challenging academic norms (don't let us stop you!), give your writing an 'uptight white person' makeover.

How to make a verb cheat sheet

Download a few published papers from scholars you admire and make a list of the verbs they use. Then cluster the verbs into three columns based on a passive-aggressive index: 'this work is great', 'this work is fine' and 'this work is terrible'. We've given you Inger's verb cheat sheet as a model below, but you're best advised to make your own.

When you're finished, stick your cheat sheet to your wall. While you are doing your literature review, examine your feelings about the work you are reading, and then pick a verb from the list that fits your judgement. Varied verb use makes your writing more interesting and precise. If you are a science student, closely examine your own verb placement and compare it to work in your discipline – could you afford to use a few more verbs? Or do you need to pare it back?

Inger's Verb Cheat Sheet example (social sciences)

Inger's verb cheat sheet (Table 2.2) will get you started, but remember every discipline is different. Hyland (2004) has a lot more examples from different fields.

Table 2.2   A verb cheat sheet

This work is awesome!	I feel neutral	This work is poor
argues	applies *ascribes*	asserts
assesses	appraises	changes
concludes	classifies	characterises
critiques	composes	chooses
deduces	contrasts	constructs
demonstrates	debates	generalises
differentiates	develops	invents
discriminates	differentiates	justifies
discusses	examines	makes
distinguishes	illustrates	recalls
evaluates	interprets	recites
examines	organises	selects
explains	outlines	states
identifies	paraphrases	tells
illustrates	performs	uses
integrates	prepares	
outlines	produces	
predicts	proposes	
proposes	relates	
proves	reports	
	restates	
	reviews	
	selects	
	separates	
	shows	
	states	
	uses	

2.6 How to use references to show who your academic network is (and isn't)

Providing references helps you avoid criticism like 'can you support this?' or 'inadequately researched', but your references do much more than that. References don't just show what sources you are quoting; they also help you position your work in relation to others. There is also a certain etiquette required in referencing, especially at PhD level. Your references should include people you want to collaborate with, and the people you hope will examine your thesis. But you can't just drop important people in to be polite; you must show how your work relates to theirs as well. This section discusses the politics of citation; we talk about using references to stand in for knowledge in the next section.

In this section, we discuss how to assemble your references. We see references acting in an enabling role, to strategically shore up your arguments. If you reference the big names in your field, then you summon the best, most robust, sources of intellectual strength to help you make an argument.

At the start of this chapter we talked about constructing an argument like a fencing match, but you can also think about academic writing as being a court of law. The examiner is the judge. You are the young prosecutor. You call witnesses (sources) to give evidence that helps build your case. You must question and dispute the stories of the witnesses and lawyers for the other side. You should do this cross-examination carefully, with all respect to the norms of the court, the niceties of the law, the views of the judge. Remember: this is a medieval court of law, not a television show. At the end of the case, the judge and jury (the examiner and your peers) must be persuaded beyond reasonable doubt that your version of events is convincing. That's all.

Thinking about the sort of people you would call as a witness to your case is the most obvious way to assemble your references, so first, call into your work evidence of people who explicitly agree with you. You may also want to call in some character references; people who can vouch for your research, method or work in general terms. You might also want an expert witness or two, people who can explain general technical knowledge that underlies your work. Finally, call in the 'opposition'; witnesses you can cross-examine who might disagree with you (but do this politely: it is a court of law!).

The court metaphor puts us on the alert for hidden seams of privilege among your witnesses and readers. Anyone who knows barristers will tell you they are a clubby lot who tend to know each other socially as well as professionally. Just like the legal profession, academia is a complex, international network of people connected in multiple ways. Academic networks are crucial to getting jobs, researching, publication, and grants – and they matter in passing your academic writing too, especially in PhD and Master's degree examinations.

In 'It's a PhD, not a Nobel Prize', Mullins and Kiley note that experienced examiners often start 'by looking at the references to see what sources have been used and whether they need to follow up on any of them. They then read from cover to cover' (2002, p. 376).

Anecdotally, many examiners start with your bibliography to see who is quoted there, including checking if their name is in it. While this might sound like an exercise in vanity, you can see it as a very sensible approach. Why did your university think the examiner a suitable expert to assess your work when their research is not relevant enough to your project to even get one citation? Inger is an experienced PhD examiner and it always irritates her out of all proportion when she does not see her name in the bibliography – it feels like a snub. You may not be in a position to know who your expert reader will be, so making an educated guess about who might be called on to examine the work is part of the work of compiling your references.

Each reference has both an academic meaning, and a significant sub-text. Who do you want to get a post-doc with? Who would you like to invite to speak at a conference you are organising? Who is editing a top journal you would like to peer review for? Citing these people helps them see how your work relates to theirs. It helps you build your network.

Demonstrating who is not in your supportive network, politely, is harder! If Professor García totally trashed your advisor's work (kind of unfairly, you think) in a recent review paper, but she's also running a very well-funded Centre of Excellence, where three of your friends work on toadstool research, you'd be well advised not to say she behaved badly in your paper. You might decide to be passive-aggressive, as suggested in Section 2.5 on verbs, or you might politely gloss over the whole thing. If you want to politely 'diss' someone in a reference, you might say something like: 'For a critical view, see García (2014)', and let the reader make up their mind. As a second example, if Professor Smith was the big name in your field 20 years ago, but continues to hold his outdated interpretation of data, you can say something like: 'Smith (1987) was a foundational contribution to the field. More recent research has followed (Li 2011, 2015).'

Likewise, if a researcher has done some extremely detailed data collection, and the results section of her most recent article is impressive, but you disagree with her interpretation of what it means in her discussion, you need to approach citing her with care. What people leave out of journal articles is often affected by length, interest, or the interests of the journal. Just because another researcher did not focus this specific research output on the exact thing you are interested in, does not mean that they necessarily disagree with you. You might say something like this:

> Araki (2016) offered comprehensive evidence, which seems to support the theory set out in this thesis. While Araki's own conclusions suggest the relevance of this data to her field of bird-elf transformations, the data can also be used to explain my research on High Elf beast magic.

And there you have it, your honour, the case for the prosecution. Go forth and prosecute your case, friends!

2.7 Using references as magic tokens to power up your writing

If you have been getting feedback like 'where does this idea come from?', 'is this your idea?' or even 'why should I believe you?!', you might need to pay more attention to your referencing strategy. We don't mean just having enough references, and formatting correctly. References are magic. They are tiny little nuggets, hidden in brackets and footnotes, that confer power and protection to researchers.

In Section 2.6, we talked about the political, personal aspects of references to show and build your academic network. References also help you write more concisely, by standing in for wider knowledge in your academic text. Experienced researchers think of references as powerful 'tokens', placeholders that demonstrate extensive research you don't want to discuss in the current work. Like magic spells, references are powerful, but they can misfire. In this section, we advise on how to avoid criticism about your choice of references.

Strategic referencing helps you establish credibility by 'leaning' on credible scholars (or by leaning on yourself if you self-cite). In a few words, sometimes just a surname and a year, you can conjure a whole argument, and then dismiss it with another name. You can take a title, and it will confer its power, prestige and authority on your argument. You can ward off criticism by festooning your claims with protective wards, footnotes, or in-text citations.

Consider the following examples of referencing magic. All these citations are made up, please don't hunt them down!

I am using 'beast magic' here in the sense recommended by Pung (2010).[1]

[1]For other uses of the term, see Scott (2012) and Ellis (2013).

While earlier scholars, like Punjabi (1976), Ascot (1981) and Rolando (1985) have suggested that spell literacy is developed through practice; more recent scholarship has followed the foundational work of Emmanuel Ashanti in *Kinds of Literacies* (1998) who first recognised that 'literacies are created through understandings' (p. 17).

Most scholars now consider that the battle was strategically of little importance to the overall objectives of the war.[2]

[2]For a recent survey of this field, see Archibald and Mbanefo (2011).

What do these sentences have in common? They demonstrate your extensive reading and your understanding of the field. References give you the power to make sweeping claims, without being criticised. With a well-chosen reference – or a cluster of them – you can gesture 'off-stage', pointing to other research that shows that you know other people might disagree with you, but you're not going to waste any of your word count or argument space on them.

Of course, you don't have to have read minutely all the other articles and books that an academic author cites. You don't want to create reference inception where you trace an idea right back to the birth of the universe. The whole academic referencing system is built on trust: if an article has been published in a reputable journal, the assumption is that the authors went through a process of peer review that ensured the quality of the work. Perusing the title and abstract, and a skim through the introduction is usually enough to see how an article situates itself, its main argument and conclusion. These kinds of references are the conference drinks party equivalent of 'Oh, yes, I once went to a paper by Professor Mbanefo – yes, I've heard of them, yes I know something about what they think.' But also, 'I once went to a paper by Professor Mbanefo which was relevant to this topic of conversation, you should look up her work!'

Since references have power, you can't use just any old citation. The researcher's name must be credible for there to be authority and knowledge embedded in it. Ask yourself the following questions:

1 Is your academic reader or examiner likely to know any of the researchers you have cited? If the scholars you are referencing aren't publishing in significant journals and presenting at major conferences, why are you citing them? Is anyone in mainstream research interested in their work? (If not, how will your own research move towards publication, conference presentations, teaching – e.g. contributions to scholarship?)

2 Is the research you cite up to date? One way to check this is to do a citation search that will tell you if any subsequent work has been built on the reference you are citing. Remember that some references are like fine wine and only gain more prestige over time, while other references might turn to vinegar.

3 Have you cited the foundational works in your field (which may date from decades, centuries or millennia)? Citing 'the greatest hits' of a discipline in a dissertation is a tricky business – too much might make your work seem archaic, not enough and you look like you skimmed!

4 Are there enough tokens? Are you relying on only a small number of names? Have you read broadly enough?

5 Have you only read academic articles when you should also have read books? Or looked at archival sources, reports, policy?

6 Do your citation choices show you have read and engaged with work that challenges your assumptions and positions?

As discussed in Section 2.6 on assembling your network, references can powerfully signal that you are not alone in having your ideas: you have important people who agree with you – including you yourself, if you have published already. It can feel odd to cite yourself, but this is a perfectly normal thing to do in academia.

You absolutely should cite your own work when relevant. Here are five situations when you should:

1 Cite your own work to acknowledge support in developing the research. An example is: 'An earlier version of this chapter was presented at the Developing Cities, Developing Poetics conference in Manchester, 2012, supported by a conference grant from Oxford Brookes University' (real quote from Katherine's PhD dissertation; Firth 2008, p. 4).
2 Cite your own work to avoid self-plagiarism. If you have previously published on a topic, you want to make it clear you are re-using a really useful explanation of your research methods, not just churning out nearly identical versions of the same research to bump up your number of outputs.
3 Self-citation helps establish your credentials. If you have been published, parts of your research have already been vetted and your ideas have been approved by reviewers and editors. Research says experienced examiners are often reassured by seeing your work has already been published somewhere else (Mullins and Kiley 2010).
4 Self-citation can save you having to do the full introduction to your research project again – you can just send people to your earlier articles, saving yourself words to dive deeper into the data, technical details, or discussion sections.
5 Finally, self-citation is normal in academia, and avoiding it suggests you are uncomfortable claiming to be an expert. Your dissertation is your claim to be an expert, so self-citation is essential.

And there you have it. Citation to give your writing a power boost. Level up!

2.8 'Do you really need all this detail?': how and when to use footnotes and appendices

Sometimes academic readers give students feedback like: 'too much information' or 'you don't need all this detail'. This feedback is confusing because it seems to run counter to the aim of academic writing. Generally, academics are seeking to provide a full explanation of a situation or phenomenon. You might think that academics thrive on lots of excess detail, but this is not the case. Academic readers are busy and want you to get to the point. Your academic reader wants enough detail to know that you know, and enough detail to understand and judge your research – but not more. Getting the right amount, and type, of detail is your challenge: not detail for the sake of it.

Leaving detail out is not the answer. Academics get annoyed when they read text that seems incomplete. You can understand this feeling. Have you ever been in a conversation where explanations of key ideas have been left out and you stand there nodding, but you have no idea what is going on? What about the opposite situation, listening to someone who fails to take into account what you know already, and boring you with patronising explanations? The overwhelming feeling in both these instances is frustration. When detail is mis-handled, there is a similar impact on the reader.

Too much detail, or the wrong kind, can create reader confusion. Part of the skill of an academic writer is to know when to give detailed explanations of our ideas and when not to. This decision is highly audience-dependent. In Chapter 4, we explain that English is a low context language; it's the writer's job to work to avoid vague-ness and help the reader understand, but you should not add extra detail at the expense of clarity. Detail is a classic 'Goldilocks dilemma': 'just right' is subjective.

We can't always anticipate what the reader already knows, so sometimes the best option is to give the reader a choice about which explanations or defi-nitions they will use. Academia has built-in features to provide these reader options and manage the detail problem: footnotes and appendixes. Most aca-demic books, like this one, will make your footnotes into endnotes, effectively making them a mini-appendix. Footnotes are more common in some disciplines than others,[1] but there is a place for them in all long-form academic writing.

When students think of footnotes, they tend to think of citation systems like Chicago or Oxford style (rather than in-text citation like Harvard, APA or MLA); but what we want to focus on here is footnoting for information. This type of footnoting is useful in any genre of academic writing to reduce reader disruption. By 'disruption' we mean bumping the reader out of the natural reading of a pas-sage to take in other information. In text, interruptions are often done by brack-eting (like this), which is a useful way to handle short interruptions, but can be both distracting and visually messy for more extensive information. Footnotes provide another space for the extra information outside the flow of your text.

When to use footnotes

Here are some situations where footnoting helps to preserve the flow of the text, while still providing the reader with any necessary information or direction:

When defining a term

If you have a lot of terms that need defining, you might make a glossary which defines key terms (we deal with glossaries in more detail in Chapter 7). Foot-notes provide a way to explain terms that need defining, but might not be used enough in the text to warrant their own glossary entry. For shorter pieces of text, or that won't include a glossary, footnotes can likewise be a great help.

Here is an example:

> The development of permanent settlements of a reasonable size in the Neo-lithic period meant that zoonoses[1] could be maintained in the population indefinitely despite causing high mortality.
>
> [1]Zoonoses, plural of Zoonosis: An infection or disease that is transmissible from animals to humans under natural conditions.

---

1   Footnotes are also common for referencing in the Arts and Humanities, particularly in History and Law. Note that this note isn't a reference – it's optional information!

When you want to provide information about just one word, the footnote number can come after the word itself. However, check your style guide as many guides prefer the footnote to come after punctuation or at the very end of the sentence.

When you are unsure if the reader already knows something

When writing for an advisor or examiner, it can be tempting to assume that they are already familiar with key concepts in your work. However, you should be making sure that your work is useful to as many people as possible, particularly if you are doing interdisciplinary research work (we discuss interdisciplinary work in more detail in Chapters 3 and 7). Footnotes can be used to give your reader the option of reading an explanation of a concept if they don't have this background information already.

Here is an example from Shaun:

> The genetic differentiation between the two lizard populations of interest was measured and it was found that the two populations were surprisingly well differentiated as evidenced by a high F_{ST} value.[2]
>
> [2]F_{ST} provides a measure of how much genetic variance can be explained by substructure within the sample. F_{ST} values near zero indicate no structure, while values nearer to one indicate that nearly all genetic variance can be explained by population structure.

To present translated material

Katherine's research often involves her translating from various European languages into English. In her field, she would include the original language in a footnote, so a reader who knew the original could check it for themselves. In fields where readers will be familiar with the languages, it is more common to quote in the original language and to include a footnoted translation.

To direct the reader to other parts of the document

In longer documents like dissertations, it is particularly easy to get lost and not remember where you read about an idea. Research also shows that examiners can jump around and read a document out of order (Mullins and Kiley 2002). Footnotes can be useful in large documents to point the reader back to relevant sections as the need arises.

Here is an example:

> As argued earlier, the rise of affordable consumer genetic ancestry testing has so thoroughly changed the practice of genealogy as to require a redefinition of the field.[3]
>
> [3]See Section 2.3 for the full version of this argument.

For interesting asides

Good academic writing doesn't 'beat around the bush' as we say in Australia – it is typically a direct style where asides and tangents are generally unwelcome. However, if an important connection occurs to you which might also interest the reader, but does not fit within the scope of your current argument, consider using a footnote.

Footnotes can also be the place to record significant ideas that arise as a by-product of your work, for example:

> Both sociologists and philosophers of biology have worked to generate theories about how human cooperation is regulated, but generally speaking there is little overlap between how these fields approach this issue.[4]
>
> [4]The work of Durkheim is perhaps an interesting exception, as his work on symbols in social cohesion is in some ways very similar to later work by philosophers.

To flag things that won't be explored further

Good academic writing typically chooses a single well-bounded argument. In the process of following an argument, the reader may have expected that some paths of enquiry would be addressed, but you did not have space, or the inclination, to pursue them. Footnotes can be used in these instances to signal which ideas will not be discussed further, or will not be discussed at all, so that the reader's mind can be put at rest.

For instance:

> This chapter will take a Marxist approach to exploring the role of the rural GP clinic as a place for negotiation of status in small towns.[5]
>
> [5]While Foucault's deconstruction of medical practice and power may seem more directly related to this line of enquiry, I wished to step back from the body of work surrounding Foucault in order to better focus on more classical ideas of class.

Good academic writing should stay on point, and be relatively easy to read. As you can see, using footnotes to supplement the context of your main text is an efficient way to maintain flow without losing the ability to define terms, explain concepts, offer direction, signal further possible paths, or flag territory left unexplored. Sometimes, however, the humble footnote is too small a tool for the task of managing extra detail. In some disciplines, like law and history, it is not uncommon to encounter pages that are more footnotes than text, but in most disciplines, footnotes are expected to be relatively short and few in number.

When to use an appendix instead of a footnote

If you find your footnotes are becoming mini-essays at the bottom of the page, it might be time to consider adding an appendix. Most universities do not count the appendixes as part of the dissertation word-count but will include footnotes. An appendix can help manage the size of your completed dissertation. Use an appendix instead of a footnote in the following situations:

1 *When you need to present a lot of (relatively unprocessed) data to support your argument*: Your argument might rest on large amounts of surprising, or hard to access, data, which is difficult for the reader to confirm independently. You may want to include tables with large amounts of information that are reproduced as diagrams and graphs elsewhere in your document. Representing large amounts of data can be a challenge (a more detailed discussion of using figures to help is given in Chapter 3). You may have performed a lot of data crunching to produce 'clean' data for processing, but feel worried about leaving this detail out. Katherine's PhD had an appendix with a scholarly edition of the full text of the lyrics she was analysing, as they were in out-of-print or unpublished works. Large numbers of maps, transcripts, images or facsimiles may also be appropriate for appendices. In the end, your decision should be based on scale and audience. If there is a lot of detail, which only some readers may want to see, the best place is probably the appendix.

2 *When you want to include extra 'back story'*: Inger remembers one dissertation that won an award because of the extra detail provided in the appendix concerning methods. In that case, the researcher was doing a study of the changing community within a fruit and vegetable market. The researcher put her diary field notes – all the times and dates she talked to people, or when a vendor moved stalls, and so on. The examiners found this information fascinating and applauded her choice to include it but not to make it 'mandated reading'. In this case, the appendix added richness and validity to the story the researcher was telling.

We have saved our most important point until the last paragraph. In a PhD examination, there is no onus on the examiner to read the appendix, so make sure your research story can stand on its own. It is highly likely readers will skip your footnotes too. If the 'extra' detail is vital to the story you are telling, try to find a way to include it in the body of your text. Alternative, irrelevant detail can be moved to a footnote on the way to being cut (as we discuss in Chapter 5).

3 'Where's your evidence for this?': using what you know to make a case

Academic English is built to make arguments. To mount a good argument, you need to have evidence and know how to use it. This chapter tackles the problem of identifying appropriate evidence and using it to convince your reader. In Chapter 2, we focused on ways to show you belong in the academic conversation – a thread that goes through the whole book. In this chapter, we deal with the other key skill of the academic writer: developing and using your 'academic judgement'.

It's important to know the rules, but it's also important to know when to break them or bend them. Every paragraph, section, figure or chapter of your dissertation is a chance to build your argument strategically. We'll show you how to find out what is 'normal' in your discipline (you might be surprised!) and how to identify the readers you are writing for, particularly your examiners. In the following sections on warrants and figures, we'll show that sometimes a stronger case is made by leaving information out of the dissertation. This chapter also includes the only 'correct' answer to a grammar question: there are right and wrong ways to use conjunctive adjectives. In this chapter, we throw around some big, philosophy and grammar words like 'epistemology' and 'conjunctive adverbs', but we also give you a bunch of practical activities to show you how to operationalise these big ideas. Often these big words boil down to just managing small details, like whether to use 'therefore' or 'however' to join sentences together.

Academic writing is where the rubber hits the road, and you need to marshal all your knowledge to construct a convincing academic argument. You'll need to include enough detail, about all your reading, field trips, experiments, interviews, analysis, coding, deciphering and counting, to be impressive, but not include so much that the reader feels bored or patronised. We help you understand how different disciplines define 'evidence' and how to move from asking a question about your topic to giving us the answer. We'll show you how to use paragraphs, warrants (reasons), conjunctive adjectives and figures to present evidence in convincing ways.

Writing experts disagree on how to write 'well', how to be 'convincing', and how to use and present evidence. Evidence is so central to academic writing that we also talked about citations in Chapter 2, and we will talk about using evidence critically in Chapter 6. This chapter may not give you the easy answer you were hoping for, but it will empower you, with clear explanations of these different opinions so that you can make strategic decisions that are right for your research project.

3.1 How to understand how different disciplines use evidence (and take advantage of it)

Is your work 'interdisciplinary', 'cross-disciplinary', or 'multidisciplinary'? These terms are used to refer to research that takes insights from one way of knowing, and applies them to another. Interdisciplinary research can be as simple as taking nursing studies insights and informing doctors; or more 'left field', like taking theories of mathematics to inform the study of poetry. There is a buzz around interdisciplinary research these days – and therefore more funding opportunities.

We all know how valuable interdisciplinary work can be. Inger did interdisciplinary research at the very start of her academic career, 20 years ago. Ten years ago, Katherine did an interdisciplinary PhD and continues to do interdisciplinary research today. And, as we write this book, Shaun is in the final stages of completing his interdisciplinary DNA science/anthropology PhD. In our collective experience, this kind of research presents difficulties for writers. In this section, we want to think about how to approach these challenges and give you some tips on producing reader-friendly text.

After you have studied, researched, and collaborated in an academic discipline for a long time, you start to use language and think about the work in a 'disciplined' way. This pun is intentional: let's think about the word 'discipline' for a moment. The *Oxford English Dictionary* defines it as 'The practice of training people to obey rules or a code of behaviour, using punishment to correct disobedience' (*OED*, online, 2018). All academics become 'disciplined' in the 'correct' way to write in their field, but the labels 'qualitative'/'quantitative' or 'science'/'humanities', describe only the most basic difference between kinds of research. In practice, what looks like a discipline from the outside does not look that way within. For example, the difference between the way biologists and physicists write can be more significant than the difference between biologists and sociologists.

As already pointed out in Chapter 2, academic disciplines have their own 'dialects', which are the end result of all this disciplining. If you are not alert to the differences between dialects, you can get caught out: the same word can take on different meanings. A word used in one discipline does not necessarily translate exactly into the dialect of another discipline. Take the word 'gender' as an example. 'Gender' is a word we use every day as a tick box on a form. Most of us understand 'gender' as a category: a way to check if we have enough women on boards, or signal to advertisers to spam you with frilly pink or ice blue merchandise (sigh). However, if you are a linguist, 'gender' means something completely different. In many European languages, 'gender' is the grammatical form of common nouns (*'la table'*, *'le chat'*). For a scientist working on animal experiments, gender and biological sex are interchangeable. For a medical professional, gender and biological sex may be different. For some social scientists, gender is understood as entirely socially constructed.

These differences in dialect are not trivial. In fact, 'gender' is one (loaded) word that illuminates the differences between whole bodies of knowledge; between models to explain the world, their theories of knowledge, officially called an 'epistemology'. Epistemologies are carefully constructed, rigorously tested, and hotly debated within a field. Within that field, what 'counts' as knowledge, evidence, logic has been agreed and workshopped in thousands of articles, experiments, analyses, and conferences. If you come along with a different way of using words, and a different way of making meaning out of them, you are likely to be met with incomprehension or confusion, if not outright hostility.

As a postgraduate student, you must learn to use the language of your primary field of research, so you can construct an argument in your discipline. The degree of difficulty only increases as you begin to try and talk across disciplines. You have to master multiple dialects and become a multicultural polyglot. Learning another new language means also learning another culture. If you do interdisciplinary work, you must be hyper-attentive to which culture you are addressing in each piece of writing. It might not be possible to produce a piece of writing that is accepted by every discipline. You may need to craft different articles, or even dissertation chapters, about the same content.

One of the consequences of doing interdisciplinary work is you may become strangely not-at-home anywhere. Katherine compares this challenge to her childhood, growing up across three continents. Crossing cultural and linguistic boundaries is difficult, but hones a lot of skills – which might be why she ended up crossing disciplinary boundaries in her research!

Exercise

Have you reflected on how your 'home' or 'first discipline' produces knowledge and how it influences what you write? Here's an exercise that might help:

- Look at Table 3.1, which has been constructed in comparative pairs.
- Try circling the idea that fits best for what your home discipline values. None of these options are 'wrong'; they just might not be how your current discipline does things.
- Note the left-hand column is 'hard' sciences and the right-hand is arts; so social scientists and humanities scholars are likely to have a mix of both columns.

Okay. Great! Now go back with another coloured pen, and circle the things valued in your 'new' or 'second' discipline. Where are they different? You'll need to do your homework to explain and defend your choices across disciplines.

Table 3.1   Table of epistemological (knowledge) differences between disciplines

Numbers	Words
Objectivity	Subjectivities
Collaborative team work	Individual insight
Detail	Big picture
The quantity of something	The quality of something
Reproducible work	Unique work
Your data	Your argument
How it relates to the physical world	How it relates to the social world
Improving a thing	Improving an idea
Work directly with materials	Work with things other people have made
Doing it first	Doing it definitively
Add your own	*Add your own*

Table 3.2   Interdisciplinary methods from Katherine's PhD

Literary studies	Musicology
Syllables	Beats
Metre	Time signature
Line	Phrase
Word	Note

In our own interdisciplinary work, we have found there can sometimes be the same epistemology, but different methodologies. For example, Katherine found both musicology and literary studies value the same kinds of evidence, but one looked at words, and the other looked at sounds. Table 3.2 explains in more detail how her methods were different.

Compare Inger's Table 7.2 in Chapter 7. This table helped Katherine identify how terms, and the long and well-established ways of analysing them, need to be explained when she moved them across the disciplinary boundaries. Making tables like this is a way of creating a 'phrase book', or tourist guide, for people from the other discipline to visit your research. The phrase book gives them just enough language to get value from the trip. The aim of your phrase book is to make sure the visitors feel welcomed and included, instead of lost and confused. You might scatter these guidebook tips through in brackets, in footnotes (see Chapter 2), or, occasionally, in an introductory paragraph. Another way to be inclusive in your writing is to include a glossary (see Chapter 7).

With careful thought and planning, your interdisciplinary guests can be welcomed into your text by the bridges you create for them. These guests are informed: they can see where you are going, and understand what is going on, even if they are not familiar with the new disciplinary landscape. Ideally, you want your interdisciplinary guest readers to see how the various knowledges complement each other and work together to explain complex, hybrid or multimodal phenomena. Hopefully, your interdisciplinary guest readers leave with their horizon broadened, and return to their home discipline with something extra, and deep admiration (and excellent feedback) for you.

3.2 How to move from having a research question to having an answer in your writing

'This is repetitive', 'why are you telling us this?'. These comments indicate a reader who is feeling lost in your manuscript; a cry for help from a reader who is swimming – or drowning – in a sea of details. Research, by its very nature, is iterative. Your questions should lead your research design; your answer or argument should inform your writing. However, if you try to capture the entire complexity of the research process as you experienced it, you are likely to end up with a confused mess of extraneous detail in chronological order; not a story with a beginning, middle and end. In this section, we discuss how all academic writing is a representation of findings, not a narrative of what happened.

Early drafts of writing, especially by doctoral students, tend to be focused on defining the research question, which is a good thing. You can't design your research if you don't know what your research question is. You will be reviewing the literature, developing a methodology and perhaps even getting started on preliminary data collection, creative work or experiments. Any of these activities will probably need to be written up in some fashion, if only to mark progress and to share it with your advisors. These bits of writing might start to look like chapters of a completed thesis, perhaps with names like 'Introduction', 'Literature Review', or 'Case Study 1'. At this stage of writing, it is tempting to think the structure of your dissertation is emerging, but we are here to tell you that these are probably not chapters yet. Early drafts almost always need to be extensively rewritten before they can be submitted, because the thesis is not the research question, but the answer to your question.

In most disciplines, having an idea about your potential answer before you start work is expected – it's called a hypothesis. Hypotheses are predictions which your research proves or disproves, and are explicit in experimental science disciplines. However, most disciplines use a form of hypothesis (anthropology and sociology are significant exceptions). A hypothesis is incredibly useful in shaping your writing and research; helping you to shape your research proposal, your research plan, your first draft. With a hypothesis, you can find a path through the research work to a potential outcome. For example, in science, a hypothesis usually suggests some easy experiments to run (at least conceptually), or factors you can test, which translate to text reasonably easily, for example: 'I tried X, and it worked. Then I tried Y, and it didn't work. Finally, I tried Z, and it worked!'

Good scientific research questions imply answers, for instance: 'we wanted to know if putting people on a calorie-reduced diet for six months affected their BMI 2 years later' has an answer embedded in the research question. This kind of hypothesis-driven research is usually a straightforward story to tell; an explorer analogy works well here. First, you start asking questions about where you are going while reading other explorers' journals, talking to the locals, and setting up your equipment. The only way to make progress is to set out, and you can only set out in one direction. You can't walk to the north and the south and the east all at once. Your hypothesis tells you to head north, to where other travellers said there was a mountain, so off you go. While you are travelling, you may meet some unexpected ravines that forced a detour, or you may find that the mountain was not where everyone thought it was, so you change course as you update your knowledge. It may be, as you do your work, you discover that your hypothesis is wrong, and that's fine. It's easier to fix a wrong hypothesis than to introduce an argument into a draft that has none. Almost always, your field is reasonably well travelled already, so you don't have to hack your way through an impenetrable jungle. Your task is more like working out a new route or going to a little-known destination. If this is the case, your expected path is mostly what you found, and it's clear what knowledge that you have discovered is actually new.

Humanities research also requires a hypothesis, but it is usually implied or assumed. The apparent exception is anthropological research, where it is considered inappropriate to go into the field work with a hypothesis (this makes anthropology and any anthropology-like research work very difficult!). Because the hypothesis in humanities research is usually implicit, students can forget to include it in their questions, leading to awkward questions that are hard to make into a dissertation, like: 'I wanted to know how kingship in Middle Earth worked'; or 'I want to know if social programs in Indonesia work to improve people's lives'; or 'I want to know what artists think about their studio spaces.'

If you start out with a question like: 'I wanted to know how kingship in Middle Earth worked', there is no implied answer, so your writing could go in any direction at all. To make a linear argument, you must generate a research question that you can actually answer, such as: 'I want to know if Ringwald's view of how Middle Earth kingship worked is supported by archival documents.' This kind of question translates much more easily to text, like this fictitious example:

Scholars have agreed for about the last 60 years that Middle Earth kingship was contingent on the support of the Silvan Elves (Baumgarden 1952, Schwartz 1992, Allan 2007, Ringwald 2014). This close analysis of seven manuscripts from the Kloster Anduin written between 1300 and 1400 will illustrate the ways in which the royal family of Naith maintained temporal power through the institutions of the Silvan Elves.

A caveat: the power of a well-framed research question is an embedded answer, but you need to make sure that your question doesn't preclude important potential findings, or make assumptions that might invalidate your conclusions. Don't make the mistake of thinking research questions must be fixed irrevocably – they are tools. You'll update your question as you continue to do your research.

Early drafts in search of a question are exploratory writing, whereas later drafts are explanatory writing. When you want to finish up your research, your exploratory writing must be translated into a research story; a difficult transition point for many PhD students particularly (and the one we deal with at Thesis Boot Camps). Going from thoughts and ideas to a polished research story is a complex task, much like trying to put together a jigsaw puzzle (with lots of sky and more than a few pieces missing!).

The first thing to realise is that the way you compile your writing does not have to mirror the order you did your research. For example, we recommend you write the introduction after the final draft of the conclusion, where you have arrived at your answers. Surprisingly, it is much easier to rewrite a text that had set off in a definitive direction, but the direction turned out to be wrong than to revise a text that had no direction at all.

Once you have a linear argument, changing direction can be successfully achieved with quite small shifts in your language, perhaps by using modifying words like 'partially' or 'in only two out of the five cases', or even 'not'. For example, you might have started out with your text about Middle Earth kingship, but when you got to the archive, it only contained letters between the prince and the lord quarrelling about money and lands. You'll need to rethink your hypothesis, but you'll find it extraordinarily easy to rewrite any draft introductions.

Building on our previous made-up example:

> *While* scholars have agreed for about the last 60 years that Middle Earth kingship was contingent on the support of the Silvan Elves (Baumgarden 1952, Schwartz 1992, Allan 2007, Ringwald 2014), this close analysis of seven manuscripts from the Kloster Anduin written between 1300 and 1400 will illustrate the ways in which the princes of Naith maintained temporal power *despite extensive opposition from* the institutions of the Silvan Elves.

Two tiny tweaks and a change of punctuation, and our argument now says something completely different. The reader doesn't need to know that you thought you were going to find something, but when you got to the archive you couldn't find it. They don't want to hear about how you spent a fortnight panicking, before talking to your advisor (who was not helpful), but a conversation with your second advisor resulted in three drafts of the new introduction, none of which were any good and then . . . Well, you get the picture! You are bored by now, and we can promise you, your examiner will be too.

Remember, the dissertation is a map to the best route to the destination of your new knowledge, not a travelogue of how you got there. When a text has no direction, we often advise students to start again with a blank page (though using your existing research, obviously!). Trying to wrestle directionless prose into a new shape is maddening. Typing up 20,000 new words is often easier and faster than reworking your existing 20,000 words into a structure. There are strategies to help you with this work, which we will outline in Chapter 4.

3.3 The almost invisible structure of paragraphs

Paragraphs should provide a mostly invisible structure to your writing. If your paragraphs are poorly thought out, you'll get feedback like 'choppy', 'disconnected' or 'structure needs attention'. Perfect paragraphs elude even the most skilled writer; there are no hard and fast rules, only guidelines. One way to improve your paragraphs is to think about each one as a mini-argument which, when connected to your other paragraphs, builds a 'chain' that leads your reader to your conclusion.

Academic arguments are made up of a kit of parts, which Booth et al (2003) summarise as a set of questions:

- What do you claim?
- What reasons support that claim?
- What principle (warrant) justifies connecting your reasons to your claim?
- What evidence supports these reasons?
- Do you acknowledge this alternative/complication, objection, and how do you respond?

How you deploy these parts is contingent on the purpose of the section or chapter you are writing. One, overly simple way to approach the problem is to treat each paragraph as a mini-argument following Booth et al.'s (2003) questions. Done this way, the first couple of sentences should be dedicated to outlining the mini-claim you are making in this paragraph and how it relates to your broader argument. You could then devote a couple of sentences to the second, third and fourth questions in Booth et al.'s list.

Should you always follow this 'mini-argument' idea and formula in every paragraph of your writing? As always, the answer is, 'sometimes'. At this advanced level, writing is not about tick-box compliance, but understanding the underlying rules and knowing how to use them (or break them). For example, standard writing advice would call the first part of Booth et al.'s formula 'the topic sentence', but in practice, you might need more than one sentence to make your knowledge claim clear. (We talk more about topic sentences in Chapter 4.)

An academic writer should always be asking themselves 'will my reader believe what I am saying?'. If you think there might be a counter-claim lurking in your reader's mind, address this directly and provide your response (consult our explanation of hedging in Chapter 6 for how to make sure you acknowledge counter-claims with the right degree of academic humility, and see the next section on warrants to decide whether you really do need to address this potential counter-claim).

If we look at examples of academic writing, we see authors break this rule all the time. Sometimes a paragraph might contain many claims and not much else, for example, here's a paragraph from the introduction of an old sociology of education paper by Inger and colleagues:

> Progress reports have become a common tool for . . . *[claim]* Practices vary from institution to institution, but most universities ask research students and their supervisors to make a written periodic report . . . *[claim]* Practices vary as to the exact composition of the reporting forms, but the progress report may also include . . . *[claim]*
>
> (Mewburn, Cuthbert and Tokareva 2014, p. 156)

We could contrast this paragraph with one from the same paper's results section:

> Paper work was seen by most of our participants as a way to . . . but the progress report, as a formal 'channel', was not used . . . *[claim]* All students in our study were reluctant to use these . . . *[evidence]* The formal channels were seen to be . . . *[evidence]* Students, supervisors and administrators all searched for ways to . . . *[evidence]* In our previous paper, we called this . . . *[evidence]* We saw the back channel as a proxy for . . . *[claim]*
>
> (Mewburn, Cuthbert and Tokareva 2014, p. 162)

Why is there such a difference between these paragraphs? In the start of the paper, the writers are trying to put forward an argument. To advance their broader argument, the authors introduce many claims at once. If they stopped to rationalise every claim, the paper would come across as uncertain and tentative. This type of rhetorical strategy is common in short journal papers.

Once the authors have 'loaded' the arguments in the reader's mind, they can spend time unpacking them in more detail. Let's contrast this example with one from the sciences:

> As communication deficits are not only common but also persistent, people with TBI . . . *[claim]* They describe everyday communicative interactions as stressful (Bracy & Douglas, 2005; Douglas & Spellacy, 2000) . . . *[claim]* Stress and anxiety are associated with difficulty expressing and comprehending a message. *[claim]*
>
> (Douglas et al. 2016, p. 1)

This introductory paragraph is, again, heavy on knowledge claims. Let's compare this early paragraph to a later one in the same paper's results section, which varies between claims and evidence:

> Self-report: Participants self-reported reduced use of . . . *[claim]* Repeated measures ANOVA with a Greenhouse-Geisser correction determined that mean frequency of . . . and this difference was commensurate with a moderate effect ($\eta_p^2 = .249$). *[evidence]* . . . Although change over time did not reach

> statistical significance ..., the measured effect ($\eta_p^2 = .148$) exceeded the recommended minimum effect size representing a practically significant effect (RMPE) (i.e., .04). *[acknowledging a limitation]*
>
> (Douglas et al. 2016, p. 8)

In the Arts and Humanities, we see a similar pattern. In Literary Studies, chapters are not split into headed sections like 'Introduction' and 'Results', instead the standard structures are implicit. Here is an extract from the early paragraphs of a book chapter by Katherine.

> The critical writings of early twentieth-century exponents of free verse, including Ezra Pound's, repeatedly called for ... *[claim]* They looked for the means to describe, ... *[claim]* One of the most useful, and least understood, of these methods was ... *[claim]* Most discussions of Pound's musical forms use ... *[claim]*
>
> (Firth 2018, p. 159)

In a later section which engages with 'close reading examples' (like the data and results sections for science papers), we see a cluster of evidence sentences:

> Extant recordings of Yeats suggest that ... *[evidence]* It is not to be inferred from the original, which ... *[evidence]* ... "The Peacock" is loosely anapaestic, ... *[evidence]* Pound follows that pattern of two dynamic stresses per line. *[evidence]*
>
> (Firth 2018, p. 170)

It is instructive to compare these different examples of academic dialects. While the kinds of evidence are different, the paragraphs tend to work in similar ways to construct arguments. Where you use evidence, claims, warrants, evidence and counter-claims will be in service of the whole. Each paragraph should, in some way, support the bigger knowledge claim you are making in that section of your work, be it a chapter or sub-section. If the overall knowledge claim is the roof of your house, you can think of the individual paragraphs as the pillars that keep it from falling. The composition and arrangement of the pillars should support the roof and be in the right proportions to be pleasing to the eye.

Exercise to make the invisible structure of paragraphs visible

Spend some time doing what we have done in this section: breaking down the paragraphs from papers you admire into their various components.

For example:

> Mewburn, Cuthbert and Tokareva (2014, p. 156),
> paragraph from the introduction:
> *[topic sentence] [claim] [claim] [claim] [claim]*

Compare paragraphs from different parts of the paper to see how the author(s) deploy the kit of parts from Booth et al. in a multitude of beautiful ways.

And then use your analysis to inform your own paragraph constructions.

3.4 What is a warrant? And how to use warrants to persuade your reader

Some of the more infuriating forms of academic feedback are the combination of 'how do you know this?' and 'you don't need to tell us this much detail'. Sometimes these two pieces of feedback are found on the same paper – why? The problem is often a lack of warrants, or not using warrants skilfully.

You provide a warrant to convince the reader that the reasons for your argument are valid. A warrant is basically a reason to accept a reason. A warrant should be, according to Booth et al. (2003), a 'common sense statement about the world that everyone considers self-evident' (p. 165). They use the example: 'Don't walk down the stairs at night because you might trip over. It's easier to trip over when it's dark' (2003, p. 170). The claim is in the first sentence, the second sentence gives a general principle behind it. According to Booth et al. (2003), warrants can take a number of forms:

- cause and effect;
- one thing is a sign of another;
- a rule of behaviour;
- a principle of reasoning.

Let's look at some specific examples of how warrants appear in academic writing – or not.

Inger has written on the experience of PhD students who have lost their advisor for some reason or other. Wisker and Robinson (2013) call these people 'doctoral orphans' and draw attention to the way they are passed around departments. Wisker and Robertson argue that doctoral orphans have unique challenges because they often end up with advisors who are not experts in their fields. Many academics avoid picking up these students, but Inger specialises in helping them and thinks they are often misunderstood. She could start to set out her argument in favour of doctoral orphans with a statement like this: *'Doctoral orphans are often better students than academics think they are.'* Inger is making a 'knowledge claim' about orphan doctoral students, but why should you believe her? You will need a reason. Inger could give you one, beginning with 'because':

> Doctoral orphans are often better students than academics think they are *because* most academics do not have direct experience of working with them.

Some people would be perfectly happy to accept such a statement, but Inger can't be sure. Remember: academic writers are in an imaginary courtroom, under cross-examination. A tricky reader might, for instance, be thinking: 'Why does an academic necessarily need direct experience to know something?' If Inger anticipates this criticism, she can shore up the reason for her argument by providing a warrant:

> Doctoral orphans are often better students than academics think they are because most academics do not have direct experience of working with them. Hearsay is not valid evidence. *[rule of behaviour warrant]*

It's ok, but a bit . . . blunt? The reader feels attacked. Let's try it again:

> Doctoral orphans are often better students than academics think they are because most academics do not have direct experience of working with them. Without direct experience, academics are forced to rely on rumour and 'what everyone knows' – which might be wrong. *[cause and effect warrant]*

That sounds better to our ear because it's a gentle suggestion. It's also reassuring to know you can shore up your knowledge claims. After all, if you can't provide a convincing warrant, it's a sign that you are on shaky ground.

In this example, however, Inger was trying to satisfy the tricky reader – but most readers are probably not that tricky. Does she need that warrant? Can she get away with the claim and a reason, without adding a reason why the reason should be accepted?

In practice, the whole warrant thing is complicated. All disciplinary communities have unique forms of 'common sense' – and like everything else about academic writing, the 'rules' must be adapted to your specific situation. Sometimes a warrant can be construed as condescending because you are telling the reader something they already know all too well. Let's go back to our original example: 'Don't walk down the stairs at night because you might trip over. It's easier to trip over when it's dark.' Most adults know that it's easy to trip when it's dark – they don't have to be told. Booth and his co-writers point out that we only need to provide a warrant like this when speaking to children. We don't want our readers – particularly our examiners – to think we are treating them like children, so leaving out the warrant can, contrary to common sense, make an argument stronger.

Remember we told you that academic writing is like being at a terribly polite dinner party? Leaving out a warrant can be a subtle signal to the reader that you are 'one of us' – part of a knowing community. If you decide most people reading the piece will hold a similar opinion to your own, you can consider leaving out the warrant and going straight from reason to evidence, like so:

> Doctoral orphans are often better students than academics think they are because most academics do not have direct experience of working with them. The data in this paper show that some 5% of doctoral candidates experience a change in supervision, but many persist in relationships which are dysfunctional.

We think this change makes the paragraph stronger, but you might be that tricky reader that doesn't agree and wants more warrant action. You can never please everyone! Ultimately, as a researcher, you need to make a judgement call about who is most likely to read and respond to the piece – and, since you are basically trying to read your reader's mind, you might get it wrong. Knowing when to leave out the warrant is like learning when it's polite at an academic dinner party to put your elbows on the table (as Katherine found from years of formal dinners in Cambridge, the answer is, sometimes, at the port and cheese stage). You develop a feel through immersion in a knowledge community, you can't learn it in advance, or all at once.

Even seasoned professionals like ourselves find warrants tricky. When developing the blog post that became this section, Inger consulted one of the best writers on writing out there, Rachael Cayley of the 'Explorations in Style' blog. Rachael remarked in an email: 'I feel like I see a lot more unstated warrants than I do explicit warrants; I often find myself asking the same question: "Can this move go unexplained in your field?".' For students who are unsure if a claim can go unexplained, Rachael thought they were still 'feeling their way'. If you find you can leave out more warrants than you were expecting, you have what Rachael calls 'growing disciplinary expertise', which may give you more confidence.

Sometimes you will be given feedback that suggests you are unconvincing or going into too much detail, or both. Feedback lets you know when you have not correctly read the reader's mind. Understanding when to give a reason for your reason (and when not to) is vital to developing an effective research argument. As hard as it can be, try to accept this contradictory feedback as an opportunity, and work on your warrants.

3.5 Signposting words: using conjunctive adverbs like 'however' correctly

Sometimes a reader will decorate your manuscript with comments like 'Hard to follow' or 'your argument isn't logical', but then can't exactly tell you why. There are lots of reasons for this, as we have covered elsewhere in this chapter and the next, but one of the less discussed reasons is problems with the way you are deploying conjunctive adverbs.

Adverbs are words that modify words or sentences by specifying a time, manner, place or degree. Conjunctions are words or phrases that bring ideas together. So, conjunctive adverbs are used by writers to create connections between ideas: within a single clause, within a sentence, or between sentences or paragraphs. We use them as transition words in 'signposting text' (text designed to guide your reader explicitly).

Signposting can be achieved by using transition words such as: 'however', 'therefore', 'furthermore', 'consequently', 'in addition', 'also', 'while'. Quite ordinary words you use all the time, right? Not really. Transition words can link together ideas and demonstrate relationships, such as similarity, consequences, effect, sequence or difference. Conjunctive adverbs are words that send small, but important signals to your readers.

You can think about a conjunctive adverb or phrase as being like a hinge in a door. Get the word right and the door will open smoothly. Get it wrong and it squeaks loudly, or opens the wrong way, annoying your reader. Conjunctive adverbs are fundamental to making sure your reader understands – and, more importantly, accepts – the arguments you are trying to make. Precision in the use of adverbs is important for everyone, but crucial in empirical research, which depends on explanations of cause and effect relationships. Imprecise use of adverbs can create confusion for the reader and make you look like a much less adept researcher than you are.

Unlike most of the writing advice we have offered so far, how scholars use conjunctive adverbs doesn't seem to vary dramatically across the disciplines. There are right and wrong ways to do a conjunctive adverb – which is a nice change! Correct use of conjunctive adverbs is a subtle thing, though, so let's look at the problem with some examples.

In each of our examples, the conjunctive adverb is used to introduce the second sentence and make it meaningfully 'stick' to the first sentence. The first shows poor use of the conjunctive adverb in a totally made-up example:

> We sequenced the coconut genome using an old baseball bat and could not identify all the elements. *Incidentally*, we changed our approach and tried using tennis balls instead.

This is wrong because 'incidentally' is a word we use to change the subject, it's another way of saying 'by the way . . .'. It would be more correct to say:

> We sequenced the coconut genome using an old baseball bat and could not identify all the elements. *Consequently,* we changed our approach and tried using tennis balls instead.

'Consequently' means 'as a result', which signals the cause-and-effect relationship implicit between the two statements. If you can't signal you understand the relationship, your reader can start to question the competence of the writer behind the words.

Most writers tend to have a limited repertoire of conjunctive adverbs, which can make your writing repetitive and limit your ability to explain relationships like cause-and-effect in your arguments. To add more variety and subtle nuance to your writing, let's try substituting other cause-and-effect conjunctive adverbs in our original, made-up sentence:

> We sequenced the coconut genome using an old baseball bat and could not identify all the elements. *Accordingly*, we changed our approach and tried using tennis balls instead.

'Accordingly' means 'appropriate to the particular circumstances', implying you think it's a logical and appropriate change. Subtle? Yes – but being a good academic writer is all about accuracy in these shades of meaning. In academic writing, the conjunctive adverbs signal to your reader that you understand the precise nature of the relationship you are talking about, giving an examiner more confidence that you know what you are doing.

The most important place to signpost using a conjunctive adjective is when you are changing direction in your argument (an issue we will also deal with in Chapter 4). If your academic writing is logical in its structure and purpose, most of the time you can assume that the appropriate transition word is implied. Simply by putting one sentence after another, you imply or claim causation, sequence or similarity. So, most of the time, words like 'furthermore', 'consequently' and 'additionally' are just 'throat clearing' (see also Section 5.6 on 'filler words' in Chapter 5).

Do, however, use conjunctive adverbs to signal when you are changing direction. Like when you are driving a car, there is no need to signal if you are going straight ahead; but we do need signals to tell us you are turning (and which way) or going to stop, and to avoid crashing into other cars who are merging into your lane. Where the similarity, consequence, effect or sequence is unclear, you should absolutely use a transition word. Use words to signal your argument is changing direction, or coming into conflict with another argument, or stopping.

We have summarised this advice in Table 3.3.

Keep the signpost words brief and unobtrusive. We don't want to focus on your turning signal, we want to focus on where your argument is going now. To avoid wordiness, use 'However' in preference to 'On the other hand'. Use 'how' in preference to 'the ways in which'.

For example:

The Senator explained the ways in which his electoral victory was unique.
vs
The Senator explained how his electoral victory was unique.

Conjunctive adverbs might sound like small details, but dissertation examiners can get very concerned about sloppiness (Mullins and Kiley 2002). Sloppiness is small errors that show you are not paying attention to the details of your writing and coherence in your argument. Your reader might start to wonder what else you are being sloppy about!

Table 3.3 When to use a conjunctive adjective, and how to know it's the right choice

Purpose of signal	Example words or phrases
You are changing direction	however, but, in contrast, on the other hand, instead, rather
Your argument is coming into conflict with another argument or position	while, whereas, conversely, nevertheless, despite, although
Your argument is about to stop	therefore, thus, in summary, to conclude, in conclusion, finally

To improve your signposting, try out the following exercise. You'll also want to read Chapter 4, where we talk more broadly about how to use signposting to help readers follow your argument.

Exercise to improve signposting words

1 Scan a page of your text and circle the conjunctive adverbs.
2 Examine each one carefully – does it precisely capture the nature of the relationship you are attempting to convey?
3 Try substituting the conjunctive adverbs with new ones which describe the same kinds of relationships – what difference does it make?

3.6 Using figures to help and not hinder

Many forms of research involve techniques that can be difficult to explain with text alone, so figures will naturally play an important role in communicating your results. Charts, graphs and plots are typical ways to display your research in these fields, but you might find yourself tempted to try to cram in too much detail and too much information into a single figure, which makes them 'crowded' or 'hard to understand'. If your academic advisors say your work is 'wordy' or 'long-winded', you might consider using more figures. Likewise, if you always struggle to stay under the word limit, your challenge is to cut words without losing meaning and find ways to condense your findings.

Remember the old saying, 'a picture is worth a thousand words'. Researchers can save on words with diagrams and graphs; often called 'figures' in the sciences. There are many types of figures you can use in research writing in addition to graphs and diagrams: timelines, Venn diagrams, flowcharts; even cartoons and memes can have a place in research writing these days. You may also think about using tables or illustrations. The advice below is mostly aimed at diagrams and graphs, but has useful general advice too.

Producing high-quality figures

Producing high-quality figures takes time and practice. Whether you are new to using graphics, or have been making them for ages and would like a refresher, here are some principles to make excellent figures.

Keep it simple

Too many variables on the one figure or graph can be difficult for readers to interpret. Try to include the minimum number of variables needed to get your point across. Where possible, use common plot formats that are familiar to viewers, such as scatter plots, bar charts, histograms, box plots, and so on. Keep text simple and away from the images. Avoid floating text on top of graphics, or putting the text in panels to make it stand out (when everything stands out, nothing does).

See our examples for how to integrate text into a figure effectively. People like symmetry and grid patterns when they are trying to digest information from a graphic, so avoid the impulse to be too creative in your layouts.

Use colours carefully

Colours are not mere decoration; they serve a purpose: to identify different datasets, indicate intensity, duration, or even danger. Avoid using strong colours in the background. Colours can change our perception of areas (i.e. lighter colours seem larger), so keep this in mind if the size of different elements in your figures matters.

Remember that people don't all see colours the same way. Colour blindness is common. There are tools available to help with colour selection to maximise visibility for people with vision impairment, which we recommend you use (a good example is 'Vischeck').[4] Seeing is not just physical; colours can have cultural meanings too, which you may want to carefully consider.

There is nothing inherently wrong with a black-and-white colour scheme. You can achieve a lot with various shades of grey to create contrast. For example, consider making trend lines a lighter shade of grey than the axis behind, to highlight the result rather than the structure of the graph.

Be consistent

If you have multiple plots in the one figure, be sure to keep the axes consistent (e.g. from 0–10 on every plot, not 0–10 on some and 0–20 on others). Try to keep graphs working the same scale at approximately the same size; this is particularly important if you want the reader to perceive them as a series. It is far better to have multiple graphs designed to be read sequentially than to try to crowd all the meaning onto one.

If you use symbols, or certain colours, for given datasets, then use these consistently across all your figures. Don't expect your readers to remember what your symbols or colours mean; use keys and legends to maintain clarity.

Clearly name, and explain the figure

All figures will need a figure number and title, and often a short explanation in the caption or figure label. Check your style guide for how to format these aspects of figures, and how and where to list them. Try to make the title clear, descriptive and distinctive. When faced with a large number of figures, it helps the reader to know they are looking at a 'Frequency histogram of housing values for a hypothetical city area', rather than just 'fig.3.a.i.i.'

Consider how to refer to the figure in your text

In fields where you are using figures creatively, think about how people are going to get from your academic writing to your image, and back to your writing again. Try to keep figures and the discussion close together. Refer the reader to the appropriate figure when you discuss it (see Figure 3.6). Your text should still make sense if the reader sees your reference, goes to check it out, and then flips back to your discussion.

Plots, graphs and charts

Figures related to statistical analysis need close attention. Many of the rules of making a strong argument in text apply to how you make a good figure: clarity; highlighting the relevant information, and knowing the unspoken assumptions of the academic discipline.

Humans are much better at perceiving lengths than we are at perceiving areas. Where possible, avoid the use of area-dependent figures. Pie charts, while common, can be difficult to interpret; almost anything that can be presented in a pie chart can be shown as a bar plot. Reserve pie charts for figures about differences in proportion.

Some plots are good for some sorts of data, but not so great for others; it might be worth trying out several plots on a beta reader to see what kind of reaction you get. 3D figures are particularly tricky. 3D pie charts, although common, add no extra value to a 2D pie chart and are the sure sign of an amateur in charge of the data. We recommend you avoid using 3D plots unless it's absolutely necessary. It is difficult, in a 3D graphic, to precisely align any given point or bar-top with the axes. Instead of a 3D scatter plot, consider offering two different 2D scatter plots; this is both easier to create and interpret.

Be sure to use clear labels on your axes and to provide units of measurement where possible – or make the units of measurement clear in your key or legend.

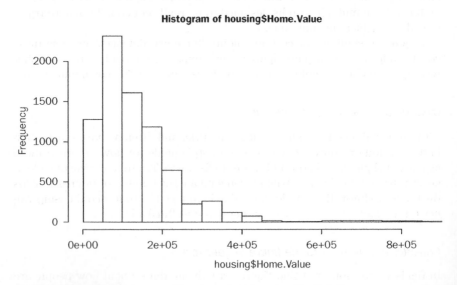

Figure 3.1 Frequency histogram of housing values for a hypothetical city area

Tweak the intervals of the points on your axes to make it as easy as possible for your audience to read the 'data story' – that might mean showing only some of the scaled data. Only use scientific notation for extremely large, unwieldy numbers. Captions should be placed below figures (though they go above tables).

See the examples below of how to label figures, and for applications of some of the principles already outlined. Figure 3.1 shows how not to use labels, while Figure 3.2 demonstrates how to use labels more effectively.

Throughout most undergraduate studies, and in many business settings, it is acceptable to generate basic figures using Excel or similar spreadsheet software. However, for academic publications, including theses, many disciplines have a preference for figures that have been generated through specialised statistical software or programming languages. Select the most useful style of figure to display your information. The plots below were all produced in R, a common statistical programming language.

See Figures 3.1–3.4 for examples of how displaying your data differently can have an impact on how useful a figure is. Figures 3.1 and 3.2 illustrate how the width of lines on a graph can impact how accurately a reader can understand the underlying information and your argument about it. Figures 3.3 and 3.4 demonstrate the differences between kinds of plotting, and how using the right kind of plot can help the reader to understand the information.

Note that the x-axis is labelled strangely in Figure 3.1 – this is because it has been made using the default 'hist' tool in R and needs to be modified. The plot

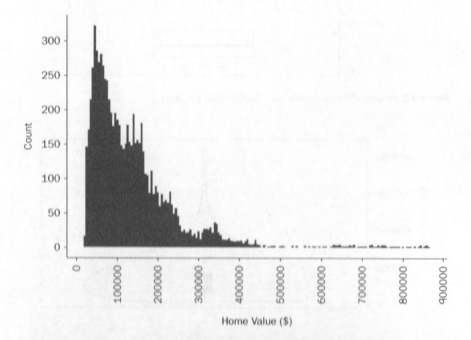

Figure 3.2 Frequency histogram of housing values for a hypothetical city area

also has a title at the top; while you might be used to putting titles here, the title and details should be with the figure caption (just as we are doing now).

Now take a look at Figure 3.2, as it is a big improvement over Figure 3.1. Figure 3.2 has used narrower bins for its frequencies than Figure 3.1, and this gives a much better picture of the shape of the distribution of the data. You should note that the x-axis label has also been fixed and the x-axis itself is now no longer in scientific notation so that it is easier to read. The title has now disappeared, as the figure caption is being used for this instead. The bars have been filled with a basic grey here as well, as it isn't necessary to see bar edges in a histogram like this.

Figure 3.3 is a basic boxplot, which is an excellent choice for showing data distributions in many cases. Here though, you can see that the data has a very

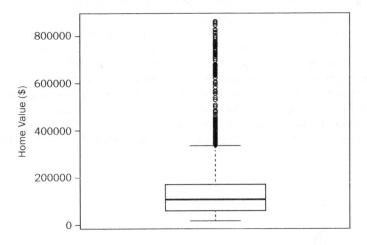

Figure 3.3 Boxplot of house values for a hypothetical city area

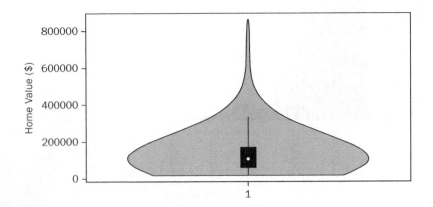

Figure 3.4 Violin plot of values for a hypothetical city area

long tail on one side that seems to be made up of small counts of high values. Maybe another kind of figure might display this more clearly; see Figure 3.4.

Instead of using a boxplot alone, we have instead used another kind of plot called a violin plot. In this case, instead of drawing dots for outlying points beyond the box plot, a violin plot uses a vertically oriented, mirrored, smoothed density plot to give a more readily understandable visualisation of the distribution of the data. A light grey colour has been added to make the distribution area stand out, but this isn't strictly necessary here.

4 'Your writing doesn't flow': making your text coherent and fluent

In this chapter, we look at some common problems of creating meaning in text and making sure your reader can follow your train of thought. If your writing is choppy, confusing, sloppy, or meandering, the reader has to work hard to understand you. They may have to disentangle confused structures, fill in gaps, re-read sections to work out what is going on or guess what you mean. Any time the reader has to do the work of constructing the meaning of your text for themselves, they are doing work you should have done. It is not in your best interest to have a reader feeling resentful, bored, lost or anxious.

Incoherent writing can be rescued. With careful editing, you can produce a dissertation where readers are eagerly turning the page to find out what comes next. The best writing allows the reader to enter a state of 'flow' – where your reader is happy to be carried along. Constructing a dissertation that 'just flows' is best described by a 'playground slide' metaphor. To construct a playground slide that is safe and fun, you need time, attention to detail, and engineering know-how. The slide needs to be high enough, but not too high; have a good slope, but not too steep; be smooth on the slide part, but with a good grip on the rungs of the ladder. When you get on a slide, all this hard work should be invisible; you should be able to simply climb the ladder, sit at the top, and let yourself go. At the end of the ride, you think 'That was fun! I'd love to do it again!'

Coherent academic writing is like a playground slide. It is well constructed, smoothly moving the reader from word to word, and sentence to sentence, and paragraph to paragraph, with no bumps or gaps. It is a straight and clear trajectory from the introduction to conclusion, making a clear argument. The reader feels completely safe in your competent writing hands, so we don't spend the whole time stopping to check the slide won't fall apart underneath us! Your reader should not have to worry about anything except coming along for the exciting ride where you explain your incredible contribution to knowledge.

This chapter helps you do the work to build that playground slide. We get into the nitty-gritty of how to create coherent writing word by word, by writing clear sentences; building from one sentence to the next; using consistent tenses; and signposting when you change direction. We also advise on some big picture techniques that help build coherence across sections or the dissertation as a whole: like free writing, reverse outlines and structural diagrams. Hopefully this chapter will help your reader put your dissertation down thinking 'That was fun! Let's do it again!'

4.1 How to make sure your reader will understand what you are trying to say

'I'm not sure what you are trying to say here', 'Do you mean "x" or "y"?', 'What is "it"?', 'Be more specific'. Reading feedback like this can be a frustrating experience. You thought your writing was crystal clear – why can't your reader understand? Feedback like this is usually academic advisor code for a bunch of problems that fall under the broader umbrella term of 'vagueness' or 'lack of clarity'.

Identifying and eliminating multiple meanings from your text is one way to improve clarity and eliminate vagueness in your scholarly English communication. Surprisingly, once you learn how to make your meaning clear, the process of editing and writing becomes more enjoyable.

Before we go on to explain some techniques to deal with vagueness, let's take a moment to understand why the English language behaves the way it does when there is ambiguity. For this, we will turn to the work of the late, great anthropologist Edward T. Hall (1976) and his concept of high- and low-context cultures. A high-context culture is one in which a listener/reader is comfortable making use of contextual information and applying their common sense to understand messages. High-context languages developed in tight-knit communities who shared a lot of experiences in common. You can think about a high-context language as being full of 'insider speak'. In a high-context language, you don't have to explain yourself too much: other people are expected to guess what you mean (cultural communication styles like this are sometimes referred to as 'reader' responsible). As it happens, many non-native-English-speaking students' first languages come from high-context environments: Chinese, Korean, Japanese, Indonesian, Thai, Arabic, and to some extent Spanish and French.

English is a low-context language environment, and this affects how readers will interpret ambiguities in your work. In a low-context culture, people rely much more on the content of the message to understand the meaning you are trying to convey. Low-context languages developed in situations where people living next to each other were different, such as in trading ports and countries that have repeatedly been colonised. Waves of invaders colonised England from the third to the twelfth centuries. First, the Romans, then the Vikings and the Normans disrupted the close bonds of the original Celtic society. As languages crowded on top of each other and mixed, people had to work harder to understand each other. It's not a good idea to leave people guessing what you mean when there are likely to be swords involved in conversations! The people of the United Kingdom then went on to colonise others, which spread the

English language throughout the world, including to Australia, where the three of us live. People have continued to adapt the English language to new cultural contexts. In fact, it is probably more correct to say there are many 'Englishes' than a singular 'English' now.

In a low-context language, the recipient of the communication is not expected to work hard to understand what they are hearing or reading. The onus is on you, the writer, to make yourself understood, which is why low-context languages are often referred to as 'writer responsible'. Writer responsible styles are common in the Germanic cultures of Northern Europe, which are themselves trader and coloniser groups, so this is hardly surprising.

Here is a small example of how this difference in context-reliance plays out in everyday speech. Let's take Japanese (high-context) and English (low-context) as our languages of comparison. Imagine two people stepping outside on a cold day. In Japanese, you can express that you feel cold by simply saying: 'cold'. Your listener will look at the situation at hand, understand that the weather is cold, and then guess that what you mean is that you feel cold. In English, you need to do much more work to make yourself understood. If you just say 'cold', your listener will probably respond with 'What's cold?'. Your English listener is not as comfortable with guessing what you mean based on context and 'common sense'. For this listener, it is not possible to know whether you meant 'I feel cold because the weather is cold' or whether you meant 'I'd like to direct your attention to the fact that the weather is cold, though I am not bothered by it.' Further, unless you make it clear by inserting a personal pronoun like 'I', it isn't clear to your listener whether you are even talking about yourself. In English, we must say 'I'm cold' or 'it's cold' if we hope to be reliably understood.

The English-speaking listener (and, by extension, reader) is likely to be confused if there is more than one meaning implied in any statement. English speakers interpret communications on a 'possibility' basis and not on a probability basis. Being 80 per cent sure that you meant 'x' is not acceptable, as there is still a possibility that you meant 'y'. This low-context situation is pushed to an extreme in academic writing because you are trying to communicate detailed information concisely and you are not physically present to answer any clarifying questions. Successful scholarly English-language communication is when each sentence has only one possible meaning.

So, if you are told your writing is vague, you are writing in a higher-context mode than the reader. You are asking them to guess what you mean when they want more certainty. Students often assume that their academic readers are experts in a topic, and so it would be rude to explain too much. Instead, expert readers in English want to be sure that you, the writer, know as much (or more) than they do.

The Commander Data technique and the 48-Hour Rule

Dealing with the vagueness problem is a matter of learning how to read your work in the ultra-low-context mode. In other words, you will need to learn to 'get out of your own head' and see your work through your reader's eyes.

Shaun likes to imagine the reader as the android character, Data from the TV show *Star Trek: The Next Generation*. Data is super-smart but likely to take everything you say literally and thus prone to making amusing errors when he interacts with humans.

Consider this exchange from the show:

Guinan: What do you think of her, Data?
Lt Cmdr Data: I find her to be a competent officer; highly motivated . . . though somewhat lacking in her understanding of the theory underlying the dilithium matrix application.
Guinan: I meant personally.

(IMDB, online)

Failing to understand the colloquial (high-context) language of his colleague, Data gives his colleague a correct, but wrong, answer. The ideal imaginary scholarly English reader is just like Data: highly intelligent and logical, but with no common sense. Data will misinterpret any multiple meaning, so work hard to make sure Data gets the message you intended.

Use the Commander Data technique in combination with the 48-Hour Rule. After you have finished writing, put aside your work for 48 hours: long enough to forget the exact words you chose, but recent enough to recall exactly what you meant to say.

With some practice, the fix for 'vagueness' trouble is quite simple. The key is to remember that you aren't writing for a clone of yourself, with all your knowledge and experiences. Nor are you writing for someone who can be relied upon to 'fill in the gaps' in what you have said. Remember, you are writing for a very low-context audience, who is detail-oriented, and reads based on possibility. Your task is to limit those possibilities so that only one meaning is possible.

Exercise to make sentences less ambiguous

Practise on sentences with multiple possible meanings; rewrite them to make different sentences with only one meaning. For example:

During the night, the cat scratched the dog with his claws.

Could be either:

During the night, the cat used his claws to scratch the dog.
or
During the night, the cat scratched the dog with the dog's own claws.

Now try the following:

- The star was observed with a telescope.
- I saw the tree coming around the hill.
- It is widely acknowledged that flying planes can be dangerous.
- I shot an elephant in my pyjamas.

Now step it up into an academic context. Here is an example based on a real thesis:

> *Some recommendations* are still relevant *and* can be implemented. *Most of the recommendations* were related to project management, public debt management, budgetary reforms and financial sector reforms.

In this case, two sets of recommendations are identified in the first sentence:

1 some recommendations, and
2 the recommendations that are relevant to be implemented.

While it may have been perfectly clear to the writer that they were referring to 2, when they said, 'Most of the recommendations . . .' in the second sentence, in our low-context mode it becomes clear that the writer could also be pointing to either set of recommendations. We can then edit the text to remove this second meaning:

> Some recommendations are still relevant and can be implemented. Most of these *still relevant recommendations* were related to project management, public debt management, budgetary reforms and financial sector reforms.

Now, go back to your work and read it in Commander Data mode, trying to identify sentences that could have more than one meaning. Treat these parts of the text for vagueness and your writing will live long and prosper!

4.2 How to write a clear sentence

'This sentence is too long', 'Write shorter sentences', 'Your sentences don't make sense' – most of us have had feedback on their writing like this at some stage of our writing career. We've often seen advice like 'write shorter sentences' given to students, but we disagree. You can, and should, write long sentences in academia, but you need to pay careful attention to the structure.

If you think about it, it's not surprising that academic sentences can become convoluted. A PhD addresses difficult, complex knowledge that will be new to the writer, and often new to the reader as well. Your task as a writer is to make your sentences as clear as possible so the reader can focus on the ideas and information, not on disentangling the structure of the sentence itself. Models from fiction (which, incidentally, is where most writing advice is aimed at) are not always helpful. When you read the prose of Marcel Proust, you often find yourself in the middle of a sentence that goes on and on; you have no idea what it's doing until you've turned the page. Great literature challenges concepts of what it is to know and pushes language to its limits. The whole point of these texts is their writing style, not their content. Proust wasn't interested in whether we understand what the narrator of *In Search of Lost Time* actually did. Proust wants us to go along for the ride as he remembers, reflects, writes and reframes his character's experiences. Literary writing is about enjoying the language. Academic writing is about understanding your research.

Usually, academic writing is bound by strict word limits. Essays are slightly easier to keep within scope, but everyone ends up having to prune their final draft of the thesis. 80,000 words (or even 40,000) might seem like an impossibly large amount right now, but once you get going, it will be surprisingly easy to go over your word limit. Writing clearly and concisely helps with the wordiness problem.

Here are eight rules to help you do that. (Katherine trimmed this list back from 10: an example of self-editing in action!).

1 Start sentences with the subject

This is both a grammatical and a logical point. Logically, the subject of your dissertation, or the subject of a section, is what most sentences should start with. Sentences that start with what's important make it obvious, right up front, what we need to know.

Grammatically, the 'subject' is the noun in the sentence that 'does' the verb. In the sentence 'I walked to the shops', 'I' am the subject: I do the walking, the shops are just there for me to walk to. In Chapter 5, we talk most about whether you should start sentences with the grammatical subject (active vs passive voice). But whenever a sentence is confused, putting the subject first will help you untangle it.

Compare the following sentences:

> As I have previously argued, it was not until after the last batch of votes was counted, that the Senator was able to declare victory.
>
> vs
>
> The Senator declared victory after the last batch of votes was counted.

We don't find out what the first sentence is really about until the end. We have to wade through some information that refers back to a previous section, and then some information about when the event happened before we can see that the sentence is actually about the Senator winning the election. The second sentence got right to the point up front. Ask yourself: What are you talking about in this sentence? Did you put that information near the beginning?

2 Use the shortest form of the word

Why say 'utilise' if you mean 'use'? Why say 'conceptualisation' if you mean 'concept'? The simpler your vocabulary, the easier it is to follow. You will need to use technical language, but if you are confusing, it helps to start with the simplest language possible and add nuance and specialist terms in subsequent edits.

Compare the following two sentences:

> The Senator promulgated his victory after the ultimate collection of democratic choices had been enumerated.
> vs
> The Senator declared victory after the last votes were counted.

'Promulgated' is a good example of words we use when we want to, as Howard Becker put it, write 'fancy' (2010, p. 9). Using the thesaurus to sound more erudite is a habit that students get into during undergraduate writing, under the mistaken assumption that sounding complicated leads to better grades. When you are writing for time-poor, highly critical academics, writing fancy can bring you more criticism than praise.

At the same time, you should bear in mind what we said in Chapter 2 about using Latinate words in preference to Old Germanic ('declared victory' is Latinate, 'said he won' doesn't sound quite so academic!). It's also worth remembering that the technical jargon might be the shortest form of saying things: tetrasodium dehydrate or parataxis aren't long words, they are technical words.

3 Keep your sentences to 25–35 words – most of the time

It's almost impossible to keep control of a sentence that's over about 40 words, and it's very hard to follow one. You really can't get lost in a 25-word sentence, as a thinker, writer or reader.

Katherine tends to run to 50-word sentences, but she has noticed that they are almost always two thoughts stuck together by an 'and' or a semi-colon. Breaking long sentences into two makes her thinking clearer, and leads to her writing being praised as 'sophisticated' instead of 'obscure'. Inger has a morbid fear of commas and tends to make sentences that are too short – leading to her writing being criticised as 'choppy'. The 25-word rule of thumb is a crude diagnostic tool, but it helps. As you edit, count the words in your sentences and try to make them 25–35 words long.

4 Try to keep to one main clause and one dependent clause

A clause is part of a sentence. You can break up a sentence into clauses by using punctuation (like parentheses, commas, colons, dashes) or by using linking words like 'or', 'and', or 'but'. You can have one clause, and then a second clause. Or you can interrupt, using commas or other parentheses, the main clause with another clause. (See what Katherine did here?) We discuss this issue of clauses at much more length in Section 5.4 on hypotaxis, but for now, we want to make the point that lots of interruptions are terrible when aiming for clear sentences, so try to avoid them where possible.

If possible, keep the number of clauses to two. Speech often uses many run-on sentences, so these longer sentences often sound quite colloquial, tentative or rambling, rather than academic. The only frequent exception to the two-clause rule is when you are setting up a list.

Let's compare these two chunks of text:

Writers find getting started on the next sentence, paragraph or chapter is often a real heave of effort. In order to avoid that heave, they might write extraordinarily long, convoluted sentences (easily a whole paragraph long), and if they can manage to have six sub-clauses, preferably broken in two by a nest of parentheses – *marked by dashes, commas and brackets – they often will (and better if they can make the paragraph last for a page or two).*

vs

Many writers find it difficult to start new sections, whether that be sentences, paragraphs or chapters. Some writers use long and complex sentences or paragraphs to avoid this difficulty.

The second chunk of text is easier to read – you might even have read the first one several times to get the meaning right. When Inger sees text like the first example in a piece of student writing, she will often say 're-parse', which is the process of breaking up a sentence into its units of meaning. When Katherine finished re-parsing the first example, she found much of the information was not needed, cutting down the example from 77 words to just 29!

We should add a caveat that all these rules can be broken in the right place and time. Break the rules once in a while for effect, but don't break them all the time, that's just tedious.

5 Keep your paragraphs to 250–300 words

We all regularly read work where the paragraph is a whole page long. Opinions vary on how long paragraphs should be. Katherine's doctoral advisor always said that you should have two or three paragraphs to a page. Inger's advisor used to say that every paragraph should be an idea, resulting in pages with many paragraphs. In dissertations in history or law, the page can consist of more footnote than text, so there's no room for even one paragraph! Generally, if your reader is marking your work, get advice on what they think is a good length. We often advise people to look at a wide range of writing in their discipline to see what is considered 'normal'.

Beyond that, it is helpful to think about what a paragraph is for. Our view is that a paragraph is not a whole idea, it's a small step in the argument. If your paragraph gets too long, the topic sentence will be something vague and hand-wavy. You should be able to hold the entirety of a paragraph in your mind at once. Check your paragraphs by trying to glance your eye over it in one sweep. Short paragraphs between long ones might indicate a piece of writing that doesn't belong in that particular section of your text; consider a footnote.

6 Don't refer back

Patrick Dunleavy, of the classic *Authoring a PhD*, claims in a Medium post: 'In a book or PhD, start each chapter cleanly. Never link back' (Dunleavy 2014, online). Dunleavy's point is that it's a waste of energy and words to start any section with 'As I discussed in the previous chapter, dum de dum de dum.' We agree with this advice. Sections of a long-form piece of writing that start by referring back, tend to send the reader backwards, in thought, and possibly literally. Forcing your reader to constantly flick a few pages back to understand what you are saying is annoying.

You want your writing to be moving forward, taking your reader along with you for the ride. So, start chapters, sections, paragraphs and sentences with the name, or noun, of the subject. Don't be shy about naming them again and again. The referring-back problem needs to be managed between sentences as well as between paragraphs and sections.

For example, compare these two extracts:

> As I have previously argued, it was not until after the last batch of votes was counted, that the Senator was able to declare victory. The Mayor made a speech of congratulation, followed by the Governor. He replied that he was looking forward to working with him in future.
> vs
> The Senator declared victory after the last batch of votes was counted. The Mayor made a speech of congratulation, followed by the Governor. The Governor said that he was looking forward to working with the Senator.

In the first example, we have trouble distinguishing which 'he' is being talked about. Generally, try to avoid using pronouns like 'he', 'she', or 'them' unless it is very obvious who is being referred to. It's less boring to re-read 'MacNeice' or 'the Senator' or 'the mycelium of pine mushrooms' than having to re-read sentences to check what 'he' or 'it' might be. See also Section 4.4 on 'themes and rhemes' for carrying a subject across more than one sentence.

7 Only explain one idea at a time

Multi-tasking in writing is very messy; try to do one thing at a time. Unlike a visual image or listening to music, where you can take in the 'whole' of multiple parts and colours/notes, you can only read one word at a time. Academic writing in particular values logical progression, explanation of cause and effect, and isolation of individual factors. If you try to discuss too many factors together, they are likely to get confused, or at least confusing. Then you'll need unnecessary words to explain them. For a more in-depth discussion of logical structure, see Chapter 4.

8 Avoid extraneous ideas

Keep to the single purpose of the writing – this is sometimes called 'the through line' or the 'narrative spine'. One simple way to find the through line is to try to think up a 'tagline' for your dissertation. A tagline is a single, dramatic sentence that encapsulates the premise of a movie. The tagline for the movie 'Alien' was 'Jaws in space'. Thinking up a tagline for your dissertation can be a helpful way to stay 'on message' in your writing. Inger did her dissertation about the kinds of hand gestures produced in architecture classrooms; her tagline was 'how architects "talk" with their hands'. Katherine's dissertation had three C's: 'Collaboration, Commission, Compromise'. As you write, ask yourself how the content fits with your tagline; if it doesn't fit, it doesn't belong in your thesis.

4.3 Use signposting to guide academic readers

'Needs editing', 'too long', 'disjointed': this feedback indicates your text is lacking in reader aids – language that helps the reader to absorb and follow the connections of your argument. In Chapter 3, we discussed using the right conjunctive adverbs. In this section, we talk about the big-picture aspects of signposting: giving your reader regular signs, so they know where they are up to, and signalling when you are changing direction.

Academics often read fast and non-linearly. Students often read slowly and linearly, so they think reading 'properly' means digesting every word. Experienced academics know there is not enough time to read and absorb every word, and that skimming, skipping and reading out of order are not wrong but efficient. Signposting is any technique that supports skimming, skipping, out-of-order reading, as well as helping the reader who is looking for clues about your position, research or credibility. Good topic sentences, section headings and the table of contents are all signposting apparatus that support a fast read-through style. Dissertation writers can expect that a more careful read-through will follow a fast skim, but in the case of articles, the first quick read may be the only time a researcher engages with your text. If your text is confusing or hard to follow, they may decide that your work isn't worth the time.

Students tutored in the North American academic writing tradition are often excellent at signposting, but for other writing cultures (English and Australian writers in particular), signposting language can seem uncomfortable, dull or didactic. Signposting language often involves repeating more or less the same information, over and over, until it seems redundant to the writer. For the reader, however, good signposting is essential. We don't want to re-read your dissertation multiple times to understand it.

Signposting happens in section headings, at the sentence level, and through vocabulary. There are three main places where you should signpost as a matter of course:

1 In the Introduction, to give the reader a 'map' of your chapter or thesis.

2 At the beginning of each section and paragraph, with a topic sentence.

3 When you are changing direction by using signposting words or conjunctive adverbs (see Chapter 3).

Signposting in the Introduction

In the Introduction, you write a 'map' for your reader. If you are doing original research, no-one has ever done this exact thing before. Your reader has never been where you have gone. You really cannot be too explicit when signposting your argument in this section. Use names, dates, genres, numbers, theories, methodologies as fully as you can to situate the research. For example:

> *In this chapter, I will discuss* the implications of fruit flies on orange production in South Australia after 1980. *First, I will outline* my use of semi-structured interviews with 60 farmers in the Tangeloville area. *After analysing these interviews* using constructivist grounded theory, *two significant findings emerge. First,* that while publicity campaigns reduced the import of fruit and therefore of fruit fly during the 1980s, the incidence of fruit fly problems in Tangeloville was perceived as constant by farmers. *Second,* that the greater public awareness of fruit fly was matched by a greater perception of risk by farmers. *This underlines the continuing importance of* agricultural industries undertaking education and publicity campaigns, *not only* in farming areas, *but more widely* across the community.

As you are reading this paragraph, you can already start to see what this chapter is going to do. In fact, you might not need to read any more than the Introduction – which is a good sign you have signposted well. A paragraph like this gives the reader a head-start on critically analysing the research: was 60 enough people to interview? Were semi-structured interviews a good way to get the information the researcher was looking for, or would a more quantitative research method have been better? Is constructivist grounded theory an effective way to analyse the data? Does that method produce the kinds of findings you suggest? Are the findings plausible from the research as described? How does this research fit into the larger thesis or argument?

Signposting through topic sentences

Academic writing is not, as we have pointed out, a murder mystery. You already know the answers, and you have told us them in the abstract and the Introduction. The topic sentence continues this practice of stating your claim and then unpacking it with evidence and analysis.

You might be familiar with different paragraph structure acronyms that mention the topic sentence, like TEEL (topic, evidence, evaluate, link), PEEL (point, evidence, exploration, link), TEXAS (topic sentence, explanation, example, analysis, summary) or PIE (point, information, explanation). Academic paragraphs need to be more sophisticated than these acronyms, but topic sentences are still crucial. Topic sentences summarise the knowledge claims and state the purpose of the paragraph, as well as, often, its conclusion. Topic sentences also link the paragraph with the larger contention, demonstrating the paragraph's relevance to the progression of the argument.

Many readers actively use topic sentences to skim. Examiners may also first skim the topic sentences of the thesis to get a sense of the shape and coherence of your dissertation, before sitting down and reading it more slowly. A well-structured thesis, signposted with strong topic sentences, should be enough to give the reader an outline of each step of your argument as it develops.

Topic sentences are not always a single sentence. Sometimes you need a couple of sentences, and sometimes you only need half a sentence. Sometimes it's better to make the second sentence in your paragraph do most of the explaining work. It's complicated: as ever, our position is writing rules are not really rules, but guidelines. Later in this chapter, we will discuss how topic sentences can be helpful in the editing process through reverse outlines (Section 4.8).

Signposting when you are changing direction

Any time your argument changes direction is a prime moment for your reader to get lost. Remember that your Introduction is like a map, and your topic sentences are like signs alongside the road. When your argument drives along this road, it needs to signal every time it is turning. You also need to know when an argument is going to stop, or when it is indicating to avoid crashing into other cars that are merging into your lane. In terms of academic writing, this means demonstrating when you are changing direction in your argument, coming to a conclusion, or dealing with conflict or confusion. We covered this in Section 3.5 on conjunctive adverbs, but sometimes we are trying to do something more complex, and a single word or phrase won't do. We might be starting a new section, perhaps approaching the issue from a new angle, perhaps addressing a side issue or a contrasting point of view. In these cases, you need a whole sentence to indicate the change, like the following two examples:

> *Having addressed the extent to which* government campaigns successfully reduced the incidence of fruit fly, *the analysis will now turn to the fact that this* reduction was not reflected in the perceptions of Tangeloville farmers.

> *While more recent scholars* including Kaffir and Yuzu (2014) and Pomelo et al. (2016) have effectively mobilised small case studies to unpack the experience of farmers in Western and Northern Australia, Satsuma (1984) and Navel (1997) have *argued that qualitative approaches have significant limitations in this field.*

Leaving out signposting information can leave your reader disoriented. Worse, leaving out information can mean the reader's assumptions run straight into your argument as it changes direction or comes to a stop, which is a messy and jolting experience for everyone. Signalling gives the reader a chance to adjust their expectations and follow you safely to your destination.

4.4 Keep your sentences moving forward with themes and rhemes

Sometimes academic readers write comments like: 'where are you going with this?' or 'This is very confusing' in page margins. Sometimes we see drafts that are punctuated with these kinds of comments for the first couple of pages before the advisor gives up and tells the person they need to 'restructure'. In some cases, it is not the overall structure that is problematic, but a sentence-level problem with what linguists call the 'textural metafunction'. Textural metafunction is a term which captures how various parts of the text – words, sentences and paragraphs – build together to make meaning. In this section, we focus on how to construct and link sentences together to convey meaning, so your text 'moves along' in an orderly fashion.

We like to think about each sentence as a piece of train track. For a train to move smoothly, the tracks need to be the same width and link to each other in an orderly fashion. Likewise, to make sentences link together, we need to pay attention to the starting and ending points and make sure there is a logical connection between them. Sentences usually start with a theme. The theme is everything in the first clause, usually up to the first verb. Here is some text adapted from one of Inger's published papers with the theme in italic text: *'PhD students who whinge* are often assumed to be "in trouble" with their candidature or supervision' (Mewburn 2011, p. 321). The first part of the sentence – the theme – indicates what the sentence is about (PhD students who moan about their circumstance). In a linguistic sense, the rest of the sentence is called the 'rheme'. Don't worry about this strange word; 'rheme' has no meaning other than to indicate every word in the sentence that is not the theme. The rheme must relate to the theme in some way, either adding information, clarification or a counterpoint. So, in the sentence above, the rheme is used to tell us that PhD student whingeing is often perceived as a symptom of something being wrong with the person themselves.

To create smooth-flowing academic text, the next sentence should 'link' to the theme or the rheme of the previous sentence. One way to make text link is to use variations of the same theme to start every sentence. For instance, here is a chunk of text where whingeing is consistently used as the theme for every sentence:

> *PhD students who whinge* are often assumed to be 'in trouble' with their candidature or supervision. *The origin of the word 'whinge'* is from the Old English word 'hwinan': the sound of arrows whizzing through the air before they strike. *The derivation of 'whinge'* suggests this kind of talk is seen as a form of 'passive warfare'. *Whingeing is a default setting* within many academic communities. *PhD students who whinge* are often assumed to be 'in trouble'. *Whingeing, while annoying to listen to for any length of time*, is not always a sign that students are actually unhappy. *People whinge* for all kinds of reasons.

These sentences notch together; neatly building on the theme of whingeing by adding variations and further information. This second example was easy to read because we do not suddenly veer away and introduce random bits of information, which require the reader to continually 'pivot' to construct the meaning as they read. Consider the effect of inserting a sentence that is related to the overall problem of student complaining that is being discussed, but does not directly pick up on the theme of whingeing (the sentence is shown in italic):

> PhD students who whinge are often assumed to be 'in trouble' with their candidature or supervision. The origin of the word ' whinge' is from the Old English word 'hwinan': the sound of arrows whizzing through the air before they strike. The derivation of 'whinge' suggests this kind of talk is seen as a form of 'passive warfare'. Whingeing is a default setting within many academic communities. PhD students who whinge are often assumed to be 'in trouble'. *PhD students in conflict with their supervisor might feel better if they can tell their story to others.* Whingeing, while annoying to listen to for any length of time, is not always a sign that students are actually unhappy. People whinge for all kinds of reasons.

When there is no connection between the themes and rhemes of consecutive sentences, it is harder for readers to follow your meaning, and therefore to follow your argument.

While using variations on the same theme to start every sentence makes highly readable text, and creates emphasis, it is not always the best strategy. Repeating the same theme can be like laying train tracks in a circle, forcing the reader to stay with the same idea. To start your train moving to the next station, try picking up on the rheme of the previous sentence instead. In the example below, we have italicised the rheme:

> PhD students who whinge are *often assumed to be 'in trouble' with their candidature or supervision*. However, PhD students in conflict with their supervisor often feel better if they can tell their story to others, so *is complaining a form of community building?* Academic communities have been accused of having a culture of complaint, which you can *experience in any kitchen on campus if you hang around long enough and listen to conversations*. Careful attention to the structure of complaining talk has shown that complaining, or *'troubles talk' serves all kinds of conversational aims*.

In this example, the rheme of the sentence before has been turned into the theme of the next sentence. When we pick up on the rheme of one sentence to make it the theme of the next, we can build new information into our argument rather than recycle old. In the text above, the story we are telling about whingeing now seems to be going somewhere.

Careful attention to how you join themes and rhemes can be used to move the reader through dense realms of information, by always introducing new ideas and concepts in relation to previous ones. Trying to consciously link the themes and rhemes of your sentences as you write is one way to start mastering the art of building persuasive arguments. At first, being aware there is this pattern underlying all academic writing can slow you down and make writing more difficult, but it is worth dwelling in the difficulty as this technique can significantly speed up your writing. If you are stuck as to what sentence to write next, look at the previous one and decide: theme or rheme?

4.5 Untangling your tenses

Whether English is your mother tongue or a second/other language, its system of tenses can be confusing. Most people with English as a first language never learn formal grammar in school and are probably totally unaware that there are four versions of the present tense! Advice like: 'write this in the present tense' is insufficiently precise to act on, especially for people who are writing a long-form piece in academic English for the first time.

For those with English as a first language, poor advice can send you to the grammar guides, only to be perplexed by the array of confusing and unfamiliar tense terms. To understand this section, you won't need to know many grammar terms, but you will need to remember that a verb is a 'doing word' (e.g. think, argue, claim, etc.). In this section, we offer advice about tense choices as well as providing a tense choice chart and simple table adapted from the very helpful Azar (2002) to help you untangle your tenses. Table 4.1 is for you to refer to as you read through the examples.

Did you know English has 12 tenses? This won't be news to those who have learned English as a second/other language, but for native speakers, it often comes as a shock. English has three 'macro tenses' – 'past, present, and future'. Each of these three has a further four subdivisions.

Your job as a writer is to pick a tense that works correctly in each sentence; Table 4.1 is a helpful guide on how to do this. If a reader has indicated that the tense you have chosen doesn't seem right, look at the chart and see if you can identify which scenario fits what you are trying to say, and try modifying the verbs in the way indicated.

Which tense should you use?

Let's start with a simple example. Let's say you are a Tolkien/Middle Earth scholar and wrote this in a discussion section of a paper:

> Li (1899) concludes that the Dunedain are a significant power in the political discourses of Gondor.

Your academic advisor tells you that the tense doesn't look right. Can you see why? In this case, your sentence contains a reference to a paper from 115 years ago. There's a good chance that this idea about the Dunedain has been challenged or disproven. (In scientific research, even 1999 would be a red flag; as always, check your discipline.) For this reason, the simple present (the tense that was used – see Table 4.1) isn't the right choice. The simple present implies a fact that retains truth indefinitely. Instead, if you look at the chart, it might make more sense to choose the tense that points to an action in the past – the simple past tense:

> Li (1899) *concluded* that the Dunedain *were* a significant power in the political discourses of Gondor.

Table 4.1 Tense choice

	Past	Present	Future
Simple	*Used for actions that were completed in the past. It uses the past form of the verb.*	*Used to refer to facts or habitual actions - things that are always true. It uses the base form of the verb.*	*Used for an action that will take place in the future. It uses 'will' plus the base form of the verb.*
	'The Algerian war **started** in 1954.'	'Most people living in Tokyo **travel** to work by train.'	'The next Olympic Games **will be** in Tokyo.'
Continuous	*Used for an ongoing action that started in the past and may have continued past a second event in the past. It uses 'was' plus the past form of the verb.*	*Used for an action that started in the past and is continuing into the future. It uses 'is' plus the 'ing' form of the verb.*	*Used for a future action that will continue through another future action or event. It uses 'will' plus 'be' and the 'ing' form of the verb.*
	'The water **was boiling** when Smith added the reagents.'	'Our lab **is working** on language acquisition.'	'The average temperature **will be falling** when we plant the seeds.'
Perfect	*Used for an action in the past that was finished before a second past action. It uses 'had' plus the past participle form of the verb.*	*Used when talking about an action in the past that has its importance in the present. It uses 'has' plus the past participle form of the verb.*	*Used for a future action that will be finished before a second future action. It uses 'will have' plus the past participle form of the verb.*
	'The defendant **had stolen** a car before he was cought robbing a bank.'	'This paper **has demonstrated** that non-state actors were important in the formation of the UN.'	'The election **will have occurred** by the time this paper is published.'

(Continued)

Table 4.1   Continued

	Past	Present	Future
Perfect Continuous	*An ongoing action in the past that was interrupted by another action in the past. It uses 'had been' plus the 'ing' version of the verb.*	*Used for an action that began in the past and has continued untill the present. It uses 'have been' plus the 'ing' form of the verb.*	*Used for an ongoing action in the future that is interrupted by another future action. It uses 'will have been' plus the 'ing' form of the verb.*
	'Jones **had been investigating** plant metabolism for 10 years when he was offered his position at the university.'	'We **have been gathering** data for the last 15 years.'	'Patients **will have been taking** the medication for 12 months when they are brought back to the clinic.'

As you can see, the choice of tense can act as a sub-text or commentary on the idea. This example demonstrates that simplistic advice about tenses should be treated with caution. It's not at all uncommon for students to get advice that a section should be written in a particular tense. Advice like this needs to be decoded carefully because it might not relate to tense choice in the strict sense. So, if you are advised to, for instance, 'write the introduction in the present tense', what it really means is you must use tenses that generally suggest action is happening in the present time. It does not mean that every verb in the introduction section must use the present tense. The technical term for this is the 'average temporal focus', which is built organically from small language 'moves' you make. Tense choices happen below the sentence level and not at the sentence level. If you ever find yourself forcing every sentence to conform with a particular set of tenses, you may have taken advice like the above too literally and will probably end up with very awkward sentences.

Before going on, it's important to dispel a myth that many writers seem to have heard: 'you can't mix tenses', or 'a sentence has to have a single tense'. This is nonsense! Sentences often have multiple verb tenses present in them, and, when done correctly, the sentence will be absolutely fine. Have a look at this example:

By preparing in advance, the armies of Gondor were able to prevail.

Check Table 4.1 to see how different tense forms are used in this sentence, but it still makes perfect sense. If you have lingering worries about mixing tenses or have been unsuccessful managing them in the past, the simplest solution is to try to write shorter, sharper sentences. The less complex the sentence, the less likely you are to put it together incorrectly.

Take a look at the example below, which we also used in our earlier section 'moving from questions to answers'. Let's imagine that the person who wrote this has been told to only write this section in the 'present tense'. Here's an incorrect version where the present tense advice has been applied too literally:

> While scholars agree for about the last 60 years that Middle Earth kingship is contingent on the support of the Silvan Elves (Baumgarden 1952, Schwartz 1992, Allan 2007, Ringwald 2014), this close analysis of 12 manuscripts from the Kloster Anduin is written between 1300 and 1400 illustrates the ways in which the princes of Naith maintain temporal power despite extensive opposition from the institutions of the Silvan Elves.

It sounds strange, right? Have a look at Table 4.1 to identify the tenses and compare it with our corrected version below:

> While scholars *have agreed* for about the last 60 years that Middle Earth kingship was contingent on the support of the Silvan Elves (Baumgarden 1952, Schwartz 1992, Allan 2007, Ringwald 2014), this close analysis of 12 manuscripts from the Kloster Anduin *written* between 1300 and 1400 *will illustrate* the ways in which the princes of Naith *maintained* temporal power despite extensive opposition from the institutions of the Silvan Elves.

English tenses can be tricky. Try to interpret the advice and feedback you get from those who aren't grammar experts with due care. Although there are more tenses than most writers realise, using them doesn't have to be hard. Keep things simple, and work step-by-step with your verbs using Table 4.1 and, hopefully, your tenses can be untangled!

4.6 How to use free or generative writing to make progress (and create flow)

'I need to see your draft', 'did you write that part yet?', 'Where is Chapter 3?!' – some advisors are desperate to get their hands on text from you! If you find the blank page intimidating, you are not alone. In this section, we offer some techniques to get your writing flowing when you are stuck. These techniques can also be helpful to produce work that 'flows' or 'coheres'.

When we are intentionally editing, we might need to use conjunctive adverbs, signposting, topic sentences, or adjust our theme/rheme progression: all of which we have dealt with elsewhere in Chapters 3 and 4. However, when we 'just write' larger chunks of text in a sustained forward flow, it can be easier to achieve a coherent and sustained forward flow for the reader too.

Generative or free writing techniques start with a clean page, few notes, and a limited amount of time (usually 10–25 minutes). The process is simple: the writer 'just writes', without stopping or editing. This type of writing is good for planning and breaking writer's block. If writing a dissertation is a marathon, generative writing is a way of warming up. Generative writing is good for first drafts where you need to be telling the story of your thesis, or first drafts of discussion, the Introduction and the Conclusion. We find generative writing promotes big-picture thinking; producing a synthesis or narrative structure, rather than a collection of small details.

Doctoral theses take a long time to write and edit. The writing must be careful, exact and backed up by data and evidence, which can make it hard to write fast. As a consequence, it's easy to start writing in a fragmented way, frequently interrupting your writing to check details or to get feedback. When you write this way, you end up with a whole lot of fragments that don't obviously fit together into a coherent piece of writing. Academic writers must adapt their writing style to the problem at hand. Generative writing is a tool bag of writing techniques to help you solve a number of different writing problems.

Building a brick wall

As noted in the Introduction, most of us are taught to write from a carefully crafted outline, intended to help us write from start to finish in a linear fashion. William Zinsser (1983, p. 97) describes his painstaking process like this:

> I have to get every paragraph as nearly right as possible before I go onto the next paragraph. I'm somewhat like a bricklayer: I build very slowly, not adding a new row until I feel that the foundation is solid enough to hold up the house.

This linear approach works best on short pieces of writing, where you can keep the whole idea in your head as you work, like a bricklayer, building each row solidly on top of the row below. While this can be an excellent strategy for essays, short stories and poems, save it for sub-sections of your thesis, rather than whole chapters. Writing like a bricklayer all the time can cause issues for long, iterative and hybrid texts like a doctoral thesis, especially if you have any interruptions, changes of plan or advisor as you go (which many people do!).

Sewing a quilt

Another approach is to attempt to sew together disparate pieces of writing into what sewing buffs call 'scrap patchwork'. Scrap patchwork is made from sewing together irregular sections of fabric, building a whole garment or a throw from a diverse ragbag of textiles and offcuts. Katherine uses the scrap patchwork metaphor because it speaks of the difficulty of this kind of writing process: trying to bind together heavy velvet with whisper-thin gauze with invisible stitching, trying to make all of these precious bits work together . . . Applied to writing you can see how this approach can make it hard to demonstrate the logic of your choices.

Rewriting afresh – 'generative writing'

'Generative writing' is a model of spontaneous or free writing first described by Peter Elbow (1998) and recommended by Robert Boice (1990) in his classic *Professors as Writers*. As Boice puts it: 'Spontaneous writing works because it puts off our internal editor, taps creative processes and allows suspension of responsibility' (1990, p. 54). It also allows us to enter that state of 'flow', defined by Nakamura and Csikszentmihályi as a psychological state where time seems to disappear, you feel empowered and like the work is intrinsically rewarding (2001, pp. 195–6).

This writing style might sound like a fantasy but is pretty easy to achieve and a great technique to master. If you struggle, you may find the structured writing exercises in Boice's book useful. You may also find the chapter on 'Shitty First Drafts' in Anne Lamott's (2007) classic *Bird by Bird* rewarding. Lamott documents how she would give herself permission to write long, boring, messy first drafts, then return the next day to radically edit it, before writing the second draft (her version of the 48-Hour Rule from earlier in this chapter). This free-form approach made her writing much faster, much less anxiety-producing, and eventually much better! We have all used generative writing ourselves and taught it in our various Thesis Boot Camp programs. This technique is tried and true and is the most effective (perhaps the only) treatment for 'writer's block' – if you give it a chance.

Free writing

Here's our recipe for planning, breaking writer's block, problem-solving or just doing a warm-up. This uses a free writing, or what Boice calls a 'spontaneous writing', technique.

1 Start with a fresh page. Some people like using pen and paper; others open a fresh page in their word processor of choice. Katherine likes to use her phone's Notes app on the tram.
2 Set a timer. Usually, 10–25 minutes is recommended (see Section 1.3 for an outline of the Pomodoro Technique).
3 Start writing. Just write. Try not to look up sources, check references or interrupt your writing. Put in placeholders if you need to, so you can come back later and add in quotes, numbers, etc. as required ('Ref?', 'Check that source!', 'Lamott Shitty First Draft chapter quote', 'use Boice here'). Don't let word choice slow you down either: put the various options/choices/ideas between slashes like we just did here and move on!
4 No one has to see the first, shitty draft of your writing, so feel free to write whatever you like! You might write the story of your thesis, to help you plan or clarify your argument. You might try to explain a complex idea in a pretend letter to your advisor. You might write about a problem you are facing.

You might just be warming up for your real writing. It's okay to write 'I don't really know where to start. This writing does not come easily. My mind is blank. What should I write about?', as long as you keep going (Boice 1990, p. 46). By the time you have reached the end of your 10-minute writing sprint, trust that your thoughts will have become clearer.

When to use generative writing in the dissertation

Generative writing, according to Boice, is slightly more structured than free writing. You will need to refer to some data, and you should have a plan. Therefore, you should have already done some careful preparation, such as making a literature review matrix (see Section 7.3) or a condensed page of notes. Generative works best for the Introduction, the Discussion and the Conclusion sections, as it promotes big-picture synthesis. It works less well for sections of the thesis which require meticulous and constant referral to the sources, like literature reviews.

For first drafts

Aim to produce a section of about 400–800 words of first draft words. Make a simple plan or statement of your argument, and collect your most significant information (probably less than half a page). Open a fresh page in your preferred writing medium. Referring only to this page, write freely for 25 minutes. Repeat.

For later drafts

Go through the tangled text of your earlier draft, extract a simple statement of the argument, and the most significant information (probably less than half a page per 500–1000 words). Sometimes Inger recommends extracting only the topic sentences of your previous drafts as starting points (see Section 4.8 on reverse outlines for a similar strategy). Open a fresh page in your preferred writing medium. Referring only to your extracted page, write freely for 25 minutes. Repeat.

Before you move on from this generative draft

Many people resist using generative writing techniques because they don't know how to turn free writing into the polished, careful academic prose that advisors and examiners expect.

Having read this book, you know that you can improve your writing. Put the draft down for 48 hours. Then go over the draft using Chapters 4 and 5 to get the writing clear. The day after that, use Chapters 2 and 3 to make sure you have included all that extra evidence, nuance and academic vocabulary you need.

We recommend generative writing as it often organically produces writing that is in the right tense, uses themes and rhemes correctly, is more clearly written, and more logically structured. Thus, you might not need to do as much editing as you expected. (You will still need to do a lot of editing.)

Generative writing works because you are writing one sentence after another, and editing in longer tranches, therefore, the sentences and ideas naturally flow into each other. Ideally, this produces text where the reader can be immersed in the flow of the argument.

Generative writing is, however, only one stage of writing. In Chapter 5 we will discuss how to fit generative writing systemically into a process of planning and thinking, writing, structural edits, and polishing your writing. We like generative writing as a way to bring enjoyment back into your experience of writing because if you find writing rewarding, it usually leads to rewarding reading.

4.7 Planning your writing with flexible techniques

Sometimes your academic readers mark up a piece of writing with arrows and circles, indicating that whole chunks of text need to be moved. Moving chunks of text is a headache for writers as it can be hard to 'stitch' the text back together. If whole sections of your writing seem to always end up in the wrong spot, you might want to rethink how you plan your writing.

Most of us are taught to plan in a linear, inflexible way which results in plans that feel more like a straitjacket than a helpful writing aid. Some people have made so many bad plans in the past, they simply give up planning altogether. This is a terrible idea. Having no plan at all is a sure way to becoming a stressed-out writer. Planning should happen before, during and sometimes even after the writing itself (as we will see in Section 4.8 on reverse outlines).

Academic writers are creative, so they need planning techniques that quickly capture the new ideas that emerge as you write. Diagrams and outlines can provide a valuable 'bird's eye view' of your thinking and can help you move ideas and concepts around, without committing lots of words to a page. This section gives you three models to flexibly plan your writing: (1) the spider diagram; (2) the thesis map; and (3) the snowflake outline.

The spider diagram

Spider diagrams work best for the early stages of planning your writing when you have more questions than answers. Spider diagrams work well for single chapters or even subsections. In a diagram, ideas are much easier to move around. The 'helicopter view' of a diagram helps you see how different pieces of writing and information might fit together. A whiteboard is the best place to make these diagrams because you can move things around and rub stuff out as your ideas evolve.

1 Start with a question or statement and draw a circle around it (Figure 4.1).
2 Draw three 'legs' out from the circle. The choice of three legs is deliberate. Humans tend to think in binary opposites (like yes/no); by expanding the possibilities to three, you are forced to think in an unfamiliar way. The small

number of legs is crucial because it helps you start to establish which questions are more important than others.

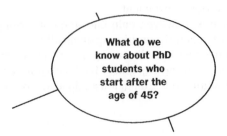

Figure 4.1 Start the spider diagram with a question or statement

3 Draw bubbles at the end of the three legs and put three more questions in them. Make sure these questions are logically related to the primary question.
4 Now, draw out more 'legs' and start to make notes about things you already know, or things you need to find out / establish; your map should now look something like Figure 4.2.

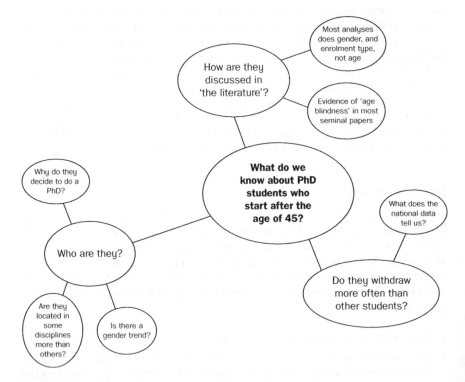

Figure 4.2 Develop the spider diagram by filling in further questions

5 Once you can see how your questions or statements relate to each other, your research should fill in the answers.
6 Keep your diagram, perhaps as a photo on your phone, or even paste the picture into your draft. Return to the diagram regularly. Re-draw it if necessary. When you find the diagram is too simple for your needs, it's probably time to move on to the thesis map.

The thesis map

A thesis map is just a table with some prompting questions that help you to 'position' each chapter of the dissertation. A map is useful to help you have a sense of where you are going, and what you need to do to get there, as we discussed in Chapter 3. We used a map when putting together this book and used it to help us include all the helpful cross-references you have encountered, as well as writing the introductions to each chapter (both forms of signposting).

Making a map is a straightforward exercise if you already have a chapter-by-chapter plan and synopsis. A map is a less-detailed, more strategic overview of the work which you can keep handy as you write. The map focuses not on the details of each paragraph, but on the overall purpose of each chapter and what you want the reader to take away with them: what do you want people to feel, think or do differently after reading your manuscript?

Treat Table 4.2 as a flexible thinking and planning tool – it is provisional. You can change or update your map at any time. Revising a thesis map helps you to reflect the progress you have made on your thinking. You may return to the whiteboard and the spider diagram to make the map. Then use the map with the next tool, the snowflake outline.

The snowflake outline

To get from a thesis map to detailed writing can be challenging. Chapters are often too big and unwieldy for useful planning – a single Humanities dissertation 'Chapter 1' might include a literature review, a methods section, an overview of the whole dissertation and more! The snowflake method helps you plan out smaller 'chunks' of writing, as advised by Kamler and Thompson (2014). Chunks are a few paragraphs or pages; substantial and analytical sections. Using a snowflake outline can help chunks become chapters, and then a whole dissertation. You can think of the snowflake outlining method as a way of planning your thesis by progressively filling in more detail. Visually it looks like Figure 4.3.

Figure 4.3 Snowflake outlines

Table 4.2 Making a thesis map

Write your answer to the following question (you might want to do this after filling in the table below).
What is the call to action: what do you want people to feel, think or do differently after reading your dissertation? Your answer
should be **150 words maximum.**
Fill in the questions in the header and the chapter columns below, adding more if you want to write into more than four chapters.
If you are doing a dissertation by compilation/publication, the chapters might be individual papers.

Introduction	Chapter 1	Chapter 2: Title	Chapter 3: Title	Chapter 4: Title	Conclusion
Please write a sentence or two summarising each of the following: Background/context to the research: The research problem statement/research gap: Aim and scope of the dissertation: Significance/contribution of the work:	**Title:** Please write a sentence or two summarising each of the following: The broad purpose of this chapter is: In a sentence, the main argument/message of this chapter is: In this chapter I will argue/demonstrate the following general points: By the end of this chapter, the reader has learned ...? (try to summarise this in a single sentence):	**Title:** Please write a sentence or two summarising each of the following: The broad purpose of this chapter is: In a sentence, the main argument/message of this chapter is: In this chapter I will argue/demonstrate the following general points: By the end of this chapter, the reader has learned ...? (try to summarise this in a single sentence):	**Title:** Please write a sentence or two summarising each of the following: The broad purpose of this chapter is: In a sentence, the main argument/message of this chapter is: In this chapter I will argue/demonstrate the following general points: By the end of this chapter, the reader has learned ...? (try to summarise this in a single sentence):	**Title:** Please write a sentence or two summarising each of the following: The broad purpose of this chapter is: In a sentence, the main argument/message of this chapter is: In this chapter I will argue/demonstrate the following general points: By the end of this chapter, the reader has learned ...? (try to summarise this in a single sentence):	Please write a sentence or two summarising each of the following: Summary of argument/main points/findings: Implications and future research:

1   Begin by using your thesis map to write a short synopsis of around 300–400 words for each of the chapters you plan to write; essentially this is an abstract for your chapter (refer to Chapter 7 for more advice on writing abstracts). Here's an example of a synopsis from Inger's dissertation:

> ### Chapter 1 The spaces of architectural education
>
> This chapter provides background for readers who might not be familiar with the history of architecture education. It explains how architectural education has developed over the last thousand years in Western Europe and how this tradition was translated in the Australian context. The chapter argues that the spaces of architectural education have always been the product of socio-material relations, from the medieval guilds to contemporary academia. This chapter argues that how and where bodies are mobilised produces different kinds of architectural subjectivities: 'master mason', 'master artist' and 'knowledge worker'.

Visually, the level of detail in this initial step of your snowflake outline looks like Figure 4.4.

Figure 4.4 Snowflake outlines start with a triangle

2   When you have the synopsis for each chapter, write a big list of everything you think should be in that chapter – data, questions, evidence, observations and thoughts. This is the creative part – enjoy! Use a whiteboard or notepad if it's more fitting. Visually your snowflake now looks like Figure 4.5.

Figure 4.5 Snowflake outlines: your triangle becomes a star

3   Review your messy lists. Start to arrange them into subheadings. Although there is no blanket rule, ideally you should have no more than two pages between each subheading, so each subheading should represent a chunk of text of about 1000 words.

Here's the list of headings from Chapter 1 of Inger's dissertation:

Subheadings in this chapter 'The spaces of architectural education'

1 The shape of the contemporary design studio
2 The medieval guild system
3 Moving into the academy
4 The Beaux Arts and Atelier
5 Articled clerks and governmentality
6 Design studio as 'knowledge generator'
7 Contemporary anxieties

(total: approximately 10,000 words)

Visually, your snowflake thesis outline now looks like Figure 4.6.

Figure 4.6 Snowflake outlines: your star becomes a rough ice crystal

Use a table format to construct a snowflake outline for your dissertation (Table 4.3).

4 From here you can use free writing and other techniques in this book to start working into each part of your thesis until it looks like a beautiful snowflake (Figure 4.7).

Figure 4.7 Your outlined snowflake is now beautiful

And there you have it.

Flexible techniques can be updated

Some people will find they want to use planning tools exactly in the order set out here (which is the way Inger gets her students to prepare for a Thesis Boot

Camp), and others will want to use just one of them. We recommend you experiment widely with planning tools, and regularly update and amend your plans. You need a flexible, powerful plan that can accommodate new and unexpected discoveries, and can grow as your knowledge of the field grows.

Table 4.3 Turning snowflake outline points into a dissertation structure

Synopsis and subheadings	Provisional word count:
Chapter Title:	
Synopsis:	
Subheadings (add more as appropriate)	
1) _____	
2) _____	
3) _____	
4) _____	
5) _____	
Chapter Title:	
Synopsis:	
Subheadings (add more as appropriate)	
1) _____	
2) _____	
3) _____	
4) _____	
5) _____	
Chapter Title:	
Synopsis:	
Subheadings (add more as appropriate)	
1) _____	
2) _____	
3) _____	
4) _____	
5) _____	
Chapter Title:	
Synopsis:	
Subheadings (add more as appropriate)	
1) _____	
2) _____	
3) _____	
4) _____	
5) _____	

Add more rows . . .

4.8 Solving illogical structures with reverse outlines

'Re-structure!' We have often seen academic advisors give students this feedback without any further instructions on why a piece needs to be re-structured or how to do it. Finding structure can be daunting. Sometimes the planned structure does not work for the final chapter, or an original draft may go through too many revisions and lose its shape. Reverse outlining – using your existing content to help make a new structure – is a technique that allows you to restructure writing after it has been written, making it flow logically again. We have all used Rachael Cayley's Reverse Outlines (from her blog 'Explorations in Style') in our teaching for years, making our own modifications to the basic idea. This section is the first time we have brought our three techniques together to form the ideal Voltron super-combined-robot version. We hope it helps you defeat your editing planet Doom!

One of the most commonly recommended ways to plan your writing in advance is to create an outline that lists the topic of each paragraph, and perhaps some evidence to include. This technique works well for a short school or undergraduate essay but is not always helpful for dissertation and book writing because the logic of writing and the logic of lists don't quite match. It's common to find, 20 paragraphs in, that your carefully made plan becomes impossible to stick to. We've all experienced the sensation of our writing plan falling apart; it's not pleasant. Don't blame yourself; the problem is the process. The plan-in-advance approach assumes that you can know everything in advance. In reality, your thinking develops as you are writing. Thinking and writing are connected; a dialogue between you and the paper/screen, as well as with editors, team-mates and advisors.

A plan or outline is a form of writing on its own, but of a different genre to an academic journal, chapter, dissertation, or conference presentation. Chapters and papers are written in sentences and paragraphs, what we might call 'full academic prose'. The act of writing academic prose has a flow to it, which allows you to express and develop certain kinds of arguments. A plan, on the other hand, is a list: a note, written in fragments. There are supposed to be lots of gaps in a plan that you later 'fill in'. The reality of academic writing is rarely as neat and straightforward as our plans suggest.

Sometimes you can update your plan, using the flexible outlines techniques in Section 4.7. Reverse outlining happens after some of the writing – or a lot – has been completed. Reverse outlining is a way of finding structure in your messy drafts. Reverse outlining is a technique that helps you deal with the different types of what Thompson and Kamler call 'disorderly writing' (2012). Three types of 'disorderly' writing respond well to the reverse outline treatment:

1 When you have a scrappy pile of bits that gestures towards being a chapter, maybe as a result of using the 'free or generative writing', as suggested in Section 4.7. At this stage, your draft might be in such disarray it

does not feel very usable. A reverse outline can help you impose some order on the mess.

2   When you have a first draft, but it's kind of a mess – at least messy enough that you feel you can't possibly show it to anyone else. Reverse outlining is a way to get this material in some provisional order – at least enough to know if the general structure and content of the section or chapter are sufficient; whether the ideas make sense; and to assess if you have done enough reading.

3   The re-writing stage, which is always long and complicated. Inger hates this part the most because she is a tidy person and editing a long, disorderly draft feels like living in a messy house. Even experienced writers radically underestimate just how much re-writing is involved in putting together a large manuscript (we radically underestimated how much would be involved in rewriting this book!). You will have to write and revise as you get feedback. The process is iterative: it is highly likely your chapters will be rewritten, reviewed and rewritten multiple times, as part of the final drafting process – and perhaps again afterwards if you have corrections! During all this writing and rewriting, you can lose the structure of the chapters. The reverse outline technique can help you find it again.

How do you do a reverse outline?

1   Identify the sentence that contains the key idea from each paragraph of your original draft (hopefully this is your topic sentence). If you can't find the key idea, or there are two, write a brief description of what the paragraph is about (or should be about) as a comment.

2   Cut and paste the sentence(s) and/or comments containing the key ideas into a new document. Read it over and decide if the order works. Rearrange it if it doesn't.

3   Read through your original draft to identify bits of text that might fit logically under each of the new topic sentences. Group related content. Cut and paste the old text into new locations.

4   When you have taken everything useful from your original draft, stop and read it over from top to bottom. Is there a coherent story emerging yet? If so, go to step 5. If not, use a highlighter to help you see the story more clearly. If you have trouble identifying the parts of the story, ask yourself the following questions:

(a) Did you pose a question or hypothesis? Have you actually addressed that hypothesis?

(b) How are you structuring your argument? (For example, is it chronological, thematic, or something else?)

(c) What are the findings or outcomes you want to prove through your writing? Can you see them in your draft?

5   Now you are happy with your storyline and your topic sentence, look at the rest of the content of each paragraph. Is the paragraph convincing? See our suggestions about paragraphs in Chapter 3.

And there you have it – a more clearly structured piece of writing. Do save your offcuts, anything that doesn't seem to belong in this draft. It may be the seed of a new project, belong in another chapter, or help out in a footnote of a later draft. This stage is not the end of your writing work, but at least your writing house is a bit tidier.

5 'Waffle': improving readability by managing your extra words

While some students struggle to produce enough words, others produce inefficient, baggy, vague drafts that are not reader-friendly. Your readers have to work hard to read a long dissertation with difficult and new concepts, they may not have enough 'buffer space' to also deal with extraneous writing. In this chapter, we teach you how to identify and eliminate 'waffle': words and phrases that don't add value.

Waffly writing has sometimes been described as needing to 'go on a diet' or 'be slimmed down' – but we disagree. We also disagree with the advice to always write in clear, short sentences, and to always avoid the passive voice. In fact, we show that some long sentences, passive voice, and padding in the text are both necessary and gracious. These techniques give the reader time to absorb and think about your information, help you to be polite (especially if you are also being critical), and give you room to be technically accurate. The purpose of cutting waffle is not to make texts that meet a generic idea of 'good writing', but to make useful, careful, correct contributions to knowledge that will edify your readers.

Sloppy writing is often conflated with sloppy thinking. Studies have shown that writing that rates well on writing clarity tests tends to be downloaded and cited more than writing that is difficult to read. On the other hand, studies have also shown that texts that were more complex to read were judged as more prestigious (Armstrong 1980). Academic writing typically is aimed at experienced and highly educated readers in the same field and must strike a balance between clarity and complexity.

Sometimes academic writers just need to delete words – to fit a word-count; to make a draft reader-friendly; because we are writing defensively; because our sentences got tangled up; or because we've been over-using some techniques. Knowing when and how to cut down on words, or add more, is a key academic skill. We'll also give you some hands-on tools to get your word count down, including a massive list of problematic words. This chapter was one of the hardest ones for us to write because we touch on some seriously nerdy grammar, but we hope close reading of this chapter will enable you to respond appropriately to people who write 'passive!' or 'grammar!' or 'horsey!' on your drafts.

5.1 Writing one whole sentence at a time

Sometimes you will get feedback that says your writing doesn't 'flow', or that your sentences seem 'clunky' or 'stiff'. Hard feedback to hear when you know the way you write sentences is slow and careful. It's demoralising when all your painstaking effort doesn't result in strong, well-made prose. In this section, we will talk about the process of writing at a granular level. We want to encourage you to write the first draft of the whole sentence in a single go, from the first word to full stop.

If you start a sentence, then stop to read an article, add a quote and a reference, check your notes, add some more words, go back and edit the start of the sentence, finish the last words and then stop, your sentence is likely to be difficult to read. When we talk to students about how they actually write, we often hear a version of this 'interrupted writing' story. Your 'interrupted writing' story might look like this:

1 Read over some notes to work out what you're going to say.
2 Check up a couple of articles and attempt to write a sentence.
3 Check over the sentence and rearrange it before entering the full bibliographic details of the reference, perhaps going to the web to double check the reference is properly formatted.
4 Have a cup of coffee. Come back and read the sentence again. Change a word.
5 Go back to a third article to check a fact; resulting in the need to change a date or detail.
6 Finally (!) move on to the next sentence. In reading over the notes for the new sentence, they note that 'articulate' would be a better word than 'explains'.
7 Go back to the first sentence and tweak it.

Imagine this process, on repeat, and you won't be surprised that dissertation writers end up with more grey hairs than they started out with. This process is what Katherine calls 'the perfect sentence vortex': a never-ending cycle of incremental improvements that means you write excruciatingly slowly and you are never satisfied with what you write.

The perfect sentence vortex leads to long and horrible sentences; a kind of 'good student' writing, which is common in students who are checking their English and students who are simply trying to write 'well'. This incremental 'bricklaying', sentence by sentence, strategy can be effective for short pieces of text (see Chapter 4). Incremental writing can also be effective in situations where getting every word right is extremely important. Katherine uses this incremental strategy both to write important emails and to write poetry; Inger uses it to write tweets and reports for committees.

If you try to 'scale up' this incremental writing, the text you produce is likely to become disjointed. The perfect sentence cycle becomes a vortex of disorderly thinking: where we keep switching brain tasks from writing, to reading, to polishing, to editing, and back again. This intellectual task switching has cognitive consequences, distracting you. You may find yourself obsessing about jobs you haven't finished yet, or having trouble with focus. Inevitably, the longer you are in the perfect sentence vortex, the slower and more ineffective you become. Task-switching (multi-tasking) is inefficient (González and Mark 2004). Most people task-switch far too often. Writing in such a fragmented way can lead to slow, painful writing, or to the kinds of tangled sentences we tried to help you fix in Chapter 3.

Writing sentences in one go is not less 'rigorous' and 'careful', it is simply more efficient. You are still doing all the tasks, but doing them in blocks (a sort of mini-Pomodoro Technique). Read and plan before you start writing your sentence(s). Rearrange and double-check after you are finished.

The best way to avoid the perfect sentence vortex is to use a writing process like POWER (Plan, Organize, Write, Edit, Revise), or Kamler and Thompson's (2012) Think, Write, Refine, Polish.

Katherine uses a diagram to explain the process in Thesis Boot Camps (Figure 5.1), and when she talks to the students she supervises, to explain how to move systemically through the stages of writing, rather than trying to messily multi-task all these actions at once.

1 Thinking is about reading, understanding, researching, analysing, or planning (see Chapter 4).
2 Writing is literally putting a word out of your brain onto the blank page and then doing it again.
3 Structural editing is where you check that your writing and your plan align, maybe using a reverse outline (see Section 4.8) to start a rewrite.
4 Polishing is all that final, careful work: checking spelling and citation styles; choosing the perfect word; deciding if that comma needs to be a semi-colon. (Inger did that work on this book and moaned about it on Twitter constantly; and then Katherine did it again, and also moaned about it on Twitter constantly. This stage always takes longer than you expect.)
5 The arrow from Polish goes back to Think: that is, you need to repeat the cycle.

You will repeat this cycle many times as you do some more researching and thinking, write another few sections or sentences, and so on, usually right up to the deadline, when you just have to hand it in. As always, your writing cycle will need to adapt to different situations and writing types. A literature review or data section needs to be carefully constructed with regular checking back to

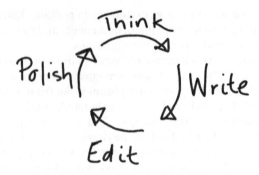

Figure 5.1 Katherine's writing cycle

the material, and will probably progress at a sentence or two at a time. On the other hand, an Introduction or discussion section can often make progress: a paragraph, or even a large section, at a time. For disciplines where these research modes are more blended (like History, Law, or Literature), these variations will take place within most chapters.

Focusing to write one sentence at a time, from beginning to end, can bring clarity and focus in your mind. This will usually lead to greater clarity and focus in your writing – and thus better understanding in your reader – and better feedback!

5.2 How and when to use the passive voice

We have seen many a student draft with sentences circled and the exclamation 'passive!' written on the top. Advisors seem to think pointing this out will help the student become a better writer (it won't). If you are a user of Microsoft Word or a machine-learning-based writing assistant software like Grammarly, you have probably noticed our non-human helpers flag every single use of the passive for editing. We love both these tools, but ignored many of their suggestions to remove the passive voice. The passive voice, like any language tool, has its uses. To rule out the passive voice altogether is not that different from banishing the hammer from your toolbox because screws are more common than nails. In this section, we outline what the passive voice is, and how it differs from the active voice. We offer a simple set of rules to help you decide where its use is appropriate.

First, some basic grammar. Here is a reminder of the ingredients of most English sentences:

Subject: The subject of a sentence is the 'doer' of the action being talked about.
Verb: A verb is a 'doing word' that denotes an action.
Object: The object is the recipient or target of an action.

Here's a simple example, with the three components labelled (this is a Shaun example, so the science is true):

| Darwin [*subject*] studied [*verb*] finches [*object*].

As you can see, in the English language we typically use the Subject-Verb-Object structure. When the subject is put at the beginning of the sentence we call this the 'active voice'. Writing in the active voice produces a straightforward and obvious sentence. Because active sentences are often clear and concise, we recommended this approach for your first draft at least (see Chapter 4).

In the passive voice, we leave the subject out, and re-order things so that the object is mentioned first; the sentence takes on an Object-Verb structure. If we rework our first example, it would look like this:

| The finches [*object*] were studied [*verb*].

In this case, there is nothing gained by leaving Darwin out. In fact, the sentence becomes less specific and less useful.

The loss of valuable detail is our main beef with the 'always use active voice' mantra mentioned above. Passive voice sentences are always a little less specific, but they should not be vague. The first thing to do when you get the 'passive!' feedback is to double check that the issue is really to do with using the passive voice. Many academics are not that well versed on the finer points of grammar and might accuse you of using the passive when you have merely been vague (refer back to Chapter 2 for more on vagueness).

You may also be thinking 'Well, I can fix the lack of specific information if I just add "by Darwin" to the end of the sentence', like so:

| The finches [*object*] were studied [*verb*] by Darwin.

All you have done here is turn a three-word sentence into a six-word one, without adding any extra meaning. Beware the urge to hang on to the passive voice: it can make your writing worse, not better.

So, when should you use the passive voice? We say any time – as a stylistic choice. However, we would recommend against it too much, because it makes your prose a bit lifeless and overlong.

Even if you try to minimise your use of the passive voice, there are three main instances where it can, and should, be used.

1 When the subject isn't known

There are times when the 'doer' in a given situation is simply not known, or maybe is unknowable. For example, if an archaeologist wanted to describe an artefact that they found in a burial site. We don't know who put the item there, so, if you followed Subject-Verb-Object in the active, you would have to say:

| Someone placed the artefact in the grave.

Not very academic! In this case, it makes more sense to say:

| The artefact had been placed in the grave.

2 When the subject is unimportant

Sometimes the 'doer' of an action is far less important than the action or the recipient of the action. For example, the building of some monumental structure, like the Burj Khalifa in Dubai. We do know precisely who designed and built the structure, but in many situations we only want to make the point that the structure was built and now exists. Compare:

| Hyder Consulting and NORR Group Consultants International Limited completed the construction of the Burj Khalifa in 2009.

with the much clearer:

| The construction of the Burj Khalifa was completed in 2009.

3 When the subject is interchangeable

It is very common in experimental academic work to describe a procedure or a set of methods used to carry out a particular research task. In these cases, the description serves as a 'blueprint' for someone else to evaluate your approach, and potentially to replicate your work. As such, the person doing the task is interchangeable; it could be you, or it could be some other person. Indeed, in large scientific research teams, the person who carried out the method might not even be one of the authors. In these situations, the following active voice statement focuses on the wrong information. It would be incorrect (and amateurish) to write:

| Barry, the lab technician, centrifuged the samples for 5 minutes.

In this case, we better appreciate the interchangeability of the subject by writing:

| The samples were centrifuged for 5 minutes.

If you are unsure, consider the ethical differences between the versions. Katherine likes to point out that some uses of the passive voice are potentially immoral. Rewriting 'The body was left on the side of the road,' as 'Dracula left the body on the side of the road,' tells a very different story!

To sum up, if you have been told to reduce your use of the passive voice, you should first determine whether or not the passive voice is really the problem. Check for vagueness. If you have been using a lot of passive voice, ask yourself whether the passive voice addresses a situation where the subject of the sentence is unknown, unimportant, or interchangeable. If it does not, then consider re-structuring to use an active-voiced Subject-Verb-Object sentence instead.

5.3 How to kill zombie words

'Too many words!', 'Boring', 'Lifeless' – this kind of feedback can indicate that you have a problem with excess nominalisation: too many verbs turned into nouns, or with too many adverbs and adjectives. Helen Sword (2012a) calls nominalisations 'zombie nouns': shuffling, half-living words. We love a good geeky metaphor, so we are running with this one. Eliminating zombie words is a way to bring your writing back to life, so sharpen your stake and load up your rifle with silver bullets, friends, but check if your zombies are friend or foe before you go on a rampage.

Sword says nominalisations are words that started life active and full of life, they used to be specific verbs (doing words) or adjectives (describing words) that got caught and had their brains sucked out by being turned into long words that sound long and important, but are abstract and often less meaningful. Sword gives an example of a zombie noun sentence: 'The prolifer-ation of nominalisations in a discursive formation may be an indication of a tendency toward pomposity and abstraction' (Sword 2012a, online). Seven nominalisations and the passive voice together made this a shuffling sentence out to eat your braaaaaaains. You probably had to read that sentence a couple of times to guess at the meaning. Sword rewrites the example, and puts it into the active voice (for more about passive voice, see Section 5.2): 'Writers who overload their sentences with nominalisations tend to sound pompous and abstract.' Sword's rewrite makes the sentence much clearer. Without zombie nouns, the sentence moves the reader forward and makes them eager for the next one.

Zombie words not only wander around in your writing, only half-alive, they also seem to proliferate when you are frightened. Too many nominalisations make your writing slow and shuffling and send exactly the wrong signals to your reader. Student texts tend to default to nominalisations because they sound 'fancy'. As Howard Becker points out, sounding 'fancy' is an anxiety response: an attempt to demonstrate how smart you are through vocabulary, rather than content (2010, p. 9). Unfortunately, this approach is likely to misfire at postgraduate level. Adjectives and adverbs can also be zombie words who suck the brains out of your writing, replacing smart, convincing texts with hand-waving, unconvincing, world-building.[5]

As zombie words, adverbs and adjectives are surplus to requirements in most non-fiction writing. Remember: adverbs are words used to describe verbs and typically end in '-ly' (e.g. quietly). Adjectives are words used to describe nouns, like 'the kind man' or 'the sunny day'. Stephen King, in his highly recommended work *On Writing*, sums up the case against with his diatribe against adverbs: 'Adverbs, like the passive voice, seem to have been created with the timid writer in mind. . . . With adverbs, the writer usually tells us he or she is afraid he/she isn't expressing himself/herself clearly' (2002, p. 118). King suggests, instead, that you try to select better verbs (we cover this in Chapter 2).

Also watch out for adjectives taking the place of evidence. V.S. Naipaul's rules for writing suggest you avoid all adjectives except those to do with colour, size and number (Kumar 2015). Replace adjectives with information: quantities, data, dates, quotes. Compare:

> The exultant Senator proudly declared victory after the very last batch of votes was counted.
>
> vs
>
> The Senator declared victory after the last batch of votes was counted at 6.20 p.m. He described himself as 'proud to have the opportunity to serve'.

As you can see, the second example is more informative, more nuanced, and it sounds more convincing. Zombie words can sound like you are making things up, rather than basing your writing on evidence, theory, scholarly engagement and expertise. A dissertation or journal article should sound more like science than science fiction.

We must add an important caveat here: not all zombie words are the same. You should never kill a word without checking whether it is friend or foe. Kamler and Thompson highlight the positive uses of nominalisation in academic texts, as a way to 'pack more information into noun groups . . . condense meanings and . . . make information more concise and foreground abstract ideas and concepts' (2014, p. 94). The next sentence includes nominalisations, adjectives and an adverb, but is a good academic sentence! The ability to choose the appropriate grammatical form of a word positively demonstrates a student is growing in academic judgement.

Ready? It's time. Let's get those zombies and write like academics instead! Try the following exercises.

Exercise 1 Adjective hunting

Go through a section of your writing and search for every time you have used an adjective to describe data. Usually, this will be a word like: 'many, diverse, extensive'. Try to replace each one by:

- a number ('7')
- date ('2016')
- name ('Medes, Persians, Parthians and Elamites')
- or approximation ('about two-thirds').

Exercise 2 Locate and examine your zombie words

Find nominalisations in your texts by searching for the suffix (addition on the end of a word):

- -ion, -ism, -ty, -ment, -ness, -ance, -ence signal probable nominalisations;
- -able, -ac, -al, -ant, -ary, -ent, -ful, -ible, -ic, -ive, -less, -ly, -ous signal adjectives and adjectives.

Pull out sentences where the words appear and experiment with 'un-nominalising' the text. Here is an example from a paper Inger wrote with her friend Rachael Pitt; we have put active verbs in brackets next to their nominalisations:

> Several job ads mentioned mobility [*mobile*], for example, a willingness [*willing*] to work from remote locations at specific times of the year and/or the ability to travel interstate and overseas.
>
> (Pitt and Mewburn 2016, p. 98)

Below we have reworked the text to include some of the active verbs – this required us to reparse the sentence, but we think the final text is more effective:

> Several job ads mentioned a desire for academics to be mobile and willing to work from remote locations at specific times of the year, and/or travel interstate and overseas.

Even published academic work can be improved, and you can clearly publish work that is full of zombie words. We only suggest you reduce them if they are impairing the understanding of your writing.

5.4 Are you suffering from parataxis or hypotaxis?

You might have heard that short sentences are better than long ones – is this advice good for academic writers?

In a word: no.

The short sentence advice may work for writers of horror novels, but academic writers are allowed – indeed, expected – to generate expansive prose, with plenty of commas, semi-colons, and so on. However, if all your sentences drag on, and on, and on . . . your readers are going to be quite tired and bored by the end of your paper or chapter.

As with the rest of life, moderation is key. The best academic texts mix up long and short sentences to create an engaging rhythm for the reader. Rhythm is important to sustaining reader attention. Varying your sentence length is one way to keep your reader fresh and interested. Short sentences create impact. Longer sentences build in pauses, letting your reader absorb your meaning, or opportunities to expand on an idea and add in more nuance.

Academic readers can find it hard to give good feedback on sentence length. If you are getting it wrong, they will use feedback words that recall physical motions. Students who write too many short sentences will be accused of being 'choppy'. On the other hand, if your sentences are too long, you might be told you are 'rambling' or 'wandering'. Alternatively, your academic reader might have their own, delightfully obscure way of telling you that the sentence length is not right. For example, Inger writes 'horsey' on sentences that are so long the reader feels like they are stuck on a runaway pony, galloping wildly about without a clear sense of direction. Katherine writes 'terse!' for short sentences that are too abrupt. Instead, Inger and Katherine could use two precise and correct words to talk about the length of sentences: parataxis and hypotaxis.

Parataxis is like this paragraph: plain English. It's one sentence. Followed by another sentence. Parataxis is direct. Your sentences are short. Perhaps too short.

Hypotaxis is like this paragraph: the use of clause after subordinate clause, which creates sentences of deeply satisfying complexity, that, even while you might get lost a little between the commas, reassure the reader that an academic of sober-minded, careful, disposition is tapping away at the keyboard crafting very polite sentences which, because of those glorious clauses and subordinate clauses, are the horsey-est (if that's actually a word) of all horsey sentences. You're on safe ground with all that hypotactic fun, believe me, because it's impossible to be too enthusiastic, or too rude, about anything when you write this way. It's no wonder, since academics love being passive aggressive (which, by the way, is the avoidance of directly saying what they think), that most 'serious' writing is full of hypotaxis.

You might have been tempted to draw a huge breath after this last paragraph – try reading it aloud and you'll see what we mean.

The sentence in English is both a unit of grammar and of oral performance. That is, there are grammar rules about sentences, but it should also be possible to read a sentence aloud and only breathe at the full stop. Even when reading silently, studies have shown that many readers move their tongues and lips as they read, this is called 'sub-vocalising' the text. Your reader must exert a physical as well as a mental effort as they scan the words on your page. Sub-vocalisation is useful for making sense of complex sentences and paragraphs, to help memorise information, or for reading a foreign language. Very long sentences are difficult to read aloud. Speed readers don't sub-vocalise; they process information in typically larger chunks – where longer sentences can be helpful. However, if the reader is moving their tongue and lips to sub-vocalise your text, and you wait too long to give them a full stop, you literally haven't given them a chance to breathe. It's the breathing which lends the sentence the sense of urgency or lulls you to sleep.

Parataxis is the breathless kind of language we use during an emergency. Too much parataxis can make your reader feel like someone has told them there is a fire somewhere and they must run away. The feeling you just created in your reader's body undermines the meaning in your text – generally academic texts are not that urgent. You can use parataxis sparingly to create emphasis, but treat it with care.

Hypotaxis, with subordinate clause after subordinate clause, makes your writing into a boring granola bar that takes way too much chewing to digest. The commas allow us to pack in lots of meaning through digressions and further elaborations, but they slow the reader down. Too many and you feel like you are wading through molasses.

One of the most common ways to clear out hypotactic sentences is to remove anything that is in parentheses. A parenthetical clause is a string of words that appears between bracketing punctuation, and offers elaboration or clarification to the main thrust of the sentence. (Parentheses is a fancy name for brackets, dashes or commas that act like brackets.) A parenthetical clause can be deleted without damaging the grammar of the overall sentence.

> It's no wonder, since academics love being passive aggressive *(which, by the way, is the avoidance of directly saying what they think)*, that most 'serious' writing is full of hypotaxis.

This example has a double parenthesis: brackets and commas! Deleting both lets the meaning shine, and the reader breathe.

> It's no wonder that most 'serious' writing is full of hypotaxis.

As we recommend in Section 4.2 on writing a clear sentence, a good academic sentence should typically be about 25–35 words long and include a main clause and a dependent clause. If you stick to this golden mean, your reader will progress at a steady, quiet, pace. However, your reader will neither feel excitement nor leisure. If in doubt, we recommend hypotaxis over parataxis. We are meant to be sober-minded academics, after all. Throw in enough parataxis to keep your reader awake and you should be fine.

5.5 Fighting weeds and cutting your word count

All academic writers occasionally struggle with word counts. Cutting words out of a long piece of writing is a difficult task; things you cut in one place start to impact things in other parts of your manuscript. It's remarkably easy to increase your word count by the time you are done 'fixing' it. If you follow our advice in other parts of this chapter, such as turning passive voice to active voice or getting rid of 'filler words' you can keep your word count minimal, but that won't help you if there is an excess content problem. If you must cut down a piece of writing for publication, or to fit within a mandated word limit for an assignment or dissertation, here are some ideas for radical word surgery.

1 Use that strike-through tool

You know – the one that does this neat thing. Back in the day, before word processors were invented, the strike-through tool was used for dealing with bits of text that weren't quite right and might need to be edited out when re-typing on paper. The strike-through function enables you to keep text where it was and use it as a reference as you write around it, perhaps trying alternative sentence constructions. You can always un-strike through if you decide the original was better and you're right back where you started.

2 Move the questionable text to the footnotes

This technique works on the principle of out of sight, out of mind. If you aren't ready to pull the trigger and kill those darlings, then the footnotes give you a half-way house to park them safely for now. By the time you come to your final polish you are usually happy to see them go, because the words clearly aren't needed any more. See Section 2.8 on when to use footnotes or an appendix for more detailed advice.

3 Start a 'maybe later' file or folder

When one of Inger's advisors, Alex Selenitsch, was doing his PhD, he kept having many ideas which weren't right for his dissertation, but they were still good. He cut and pasted these ideas into a new document and stashed them in his 'maybe later' folder. Inger started a 'maybe later' folder years ago, but has yet to dip into it and resurrect any of the bits of writing stashed there. Katherine called her file the 'PhD Cull' and later dug out material for articles and advising researcher students. The 'maybe later' folder is a bit like the footnotes: an ideas graveyard where unwanted text can rest in peace, but without being deleted permanently.

4 Prune the overhanging branches

Writing a large document is a bit like owning a garden: some parts can get overgrown and need pruning. Sometimes taking out a whole chapter or section makes more sense than trying to nip little bits out from all over the place. A good dissertation is a highly integrated text – all the various parts rely on each other to a greater or lesser extent. If you find a section that is not as integrated as the others, this is a sign that it doesn't need to be in this specific bit of writing. At the end of a PhD, it is common to start on another chapter that should be the start of your post-doc project, not the end of your dissertation. Inger nearly wrote another chapter on online learning at the end of her dissertation on hand gestures. Looking back, this seems ridiculous, but she vividly remembers the idea making total sense at the time. Katherine calls this problem 'herniation', where your current project 'blows out' with an interest-ing, but not directly relevant, digression. She has a co-author who typically starts his next article with a blow-out from the middle of a previous article. Cutting thousands of words out returns the current article to its proper size and structure and gives him the seed for the next one. You can always think about moving the text to the appendix if it isn't right for a 'later' file or project. (For more on appendixes, see Section 2.8.)

5 Squeeze out excess words from your text

Squeeze out unneeded words by putting brackets around words and phrases that you don't need. Look for areas were two words can become one, or where the words can be eliminated altogether. This technique is adapted from Zinsser's *On Writing Well* (1983) and is a respectful way to edit other people's work, highlighting problematic areas, without forcing a solution. For example:

> All writers (will have to) edit their prose, but (the) great writers edit (it) viciously, always trying to eliminate (words which are) 'fuzz' – (excess) words (which are not adding anything of value). Zinsser compares (the process of editing out) 'fuzz' to fighting weeds – you will always be slightly behind (because they creep in when you aren't looking for them). (One of my (pet) hates is (the word)) 'also'. (If you search and) replace all instances (of this word) (you will find you can live without it and) your writing will improve (instantly). (Likewise, the word) 'very'.

Let's try that again:

> All writers edit their prose, but great writers edit viciously. The point of editing is to eliminate 'fuzz', or excess words which don't add value. Zinsser compares removing 'fuzz' to fighting weeds – you will always be slightly behind. Two examples of fuzz are 'also' and 'very'. Work at keeping them out of your text and your writing will improve.

The lesson in all this? Excess in early drafts is normal and you need to get comfortable using the delete key. It's hard to write concisely on a subject if you don't understand it clearly. Sometimes the only way to get to the idea is to write it out in a messy and overly-verbose way in your first drafts. It's likely that you will generate far more text than you should use. It can be tempting to keep this excess to 'dress up' your writing to appear more intelligent, or to pad out your word count. Resist the urge. The ideas and findings of a dissertation are important; a padded word count looks like you are hiding weak research.

Cultivating a simple and precise writing style is like painting your walls white – a backdrop against which your ideas can stand out in colour. It can be hard, emotionally draining work to do the necessary word pruning, but remember that examiners are likely to view a streamlined dissertation as a sign that you are confident and in charge of your material.

5.6 Get rid of filler words

Is your writing described as 'woolly', 'waffly', 'soft', 'cluttered', 'baggy', 'windy', 'verbose' or 'muddy'? Are you hundreds (or thousands) of words over your word count, but instead of half-writing the next book by mistake (as we talked about in Section 5.5), you just have loads of dead wood? Are you nervous about putting forward your ideas and so avoid saying what you think by putting a pillow of nice, soft, careful, words between you and the reader? If you related to anything we have said so far, you have a problem with filler words. In this section, we explain what filler words are and provide you with a list of the most common words and phrases. You can use this list to search and destroy pesky filler words in your text.

Filler words (or pleonasms) are common words or phrases which creep into your writing without your conscious awareness. The problem with filler words is they add to the word count without making more meaning. While some of these fillers are conventional, many filler words are pointless 'stuffing' that can be eliminated from your writing without losing meaning. Many filler words are the equivalent of 'um' or 'uh' in speech: they keep the words moving while giving us a second or two to think about what is coming next. Katherine and Inger do add these filler words when they're writing blog posts, to slow down the pace of dense information and to sound more conversational. However, an academic dissertation is supposed to be dense and formal. Katherine finds getting started on the next sentence often a real effort, so she frequently starts a sentence with an unnecessary filler word, like 'Furthermore', which is great for drafting, because it keeps the words flowing. However, if you fall into this starter-word habit, you will need to be aware it has happened and delete the filler when you are polishing up your writing.

Working out what is, and what is not, a filler in your writing can be tricky. There are lots of stock phrases that we use to connect sentences, signpost, and change direction; words like 'however', 'therefore', 'thus', 'in comparison' and so on (see Chapters 3 and 4). Filler words can also be longer phrases, like 'Olearius makes clear' or 'In order to understand this phenomenon we must first assess . . .'. These words and phrases are handy, but if they appear in every other sentence, they are just padding out your writing.

Some writers use questions as fillers too. If starting your paragraph with your research question makes it easier to draft a coherent reply, then go for it! Just make sure to take the questions out before you hand them in.

On the subject of questions, Katherine is of the opinion that you should not use them in a dissertation. It is the job of the examiner to ask the questions, it is the job of the student to answer them. When you are a student, following Katherine's advice on questions is the safe strategy, but when you have graduated, you might want to think about adjusting your style appropriately.[6]

Not all stuffing words are a problem. All academic writers use stuffing words, called 'hedging' terms, to imply uncertainty (even if we aren't really uncertain – we'll get to that in Chapter 6). Stuffing words in these places give you some cushioning room: acknowledging that scholarly thinking will advance beyond your conclusions; to note that your results are 'strongly probable' rather than 'true'; or to disagree with another scholar without being brutal. Think of academic writing as an aerodynamic office chair. You don't want so many filler words that your writing is 'soft', 'baggy', 'cluttered' – but everyone does appreciate a little bit of cushioning on the seat!

Fortunately, search and replace makes it easy to find all your excessive 'moreover' and 'makes clear', and either delete the phrase, or replace it with 'therefore', 'additionally', or 'explains', 'claims', when you get to that final polishing stage of writing.

Exercise 1 Search and destroy list of filler words (or words that may be filler words if over-used)

Use the list below to search for filler words you might be over-using in your text. Before destroying them, though, remember to ask: 'Are you friend or foe?'.

> among
> amongst
> it
> that
> this
> throughout
> whether or not
> which
> within

Look out for phrases that include:

> of the, to the, on the, in the, at the (or of this etc.)
> in, by, for, at, on, of (especially in phrases like 'of the' or 'at this')
> there is, there are, there were

Look out for phrases that use:

> 'able' or 'ability' (is able to, may have the ability to)
> any form of 'shall' (should), use 'will'
> 'am, is, are, was, were, be, and been' can suggest passive language, rather than active verbs
> to do (or any other infinitive verb forms as these are often used in passive or conditional verb forms)
> is going to

These words and phrases constitute another danger area:

> a brief discussion of/around
> at this point in time
> different
> end result
> fascinating
> final conclusions
> final outcome
> first and foremost
> for the purpose of
> I would describe this methodology as having

important
in order to
it is at this point
multifaceted
previous mentions in this dissertation
relates to a number of different ideas
resulted in
varied
various
we must, it is essential to
when it comes to
with reference to

Watch out for:

concept
conceptualisation
idea
notion

Two other areas for filler words are:

1. nominalisations (see Chapter 5): anything with the suffix -ion, -ism, -ty, -ment, -ness, -ance, -ence.
2. adjectives: anything with the suffix (addition on the end of a word) -able, -ac, -al, -ant, -ary, -ent, -ful, -ible, -ic, -ive, -less, -ly, -ous.

6 'Uncritical!': taking a stand in your writing

This chapter presents tactics and strategies for increasing the strength of your analysis through writing, as well as showing how to discuss the limitations of other people's work respectfully. By the end of this chapter, you should feel more confident about dealing with feedback about your writing being 'uncritical' or 'descriptive'.

At postgraduate level, writers must take command of their materials and provide explanations and interpretations of the data they are presenting. Sometimes student writing is criticised as 'too soft' or not argumentative enough. Often the problem stems from too much reporting and not enough evaluating. In this section, we will discuss how to provide additional critique that will convince the reader that there is an expert in charge of the text.

It can be a big shift to recognise that you have the knowledge, authority and ability to challenge the ideas of even the most senior thinkers in your field. It's important to grasp the scholarly nettle because you are expected to challenge the ideas of other published researchers – but do it politely! This chapter encourages you to replace reverence for authority with even-handed analysis; critique other people's writing with generosity; and make sure you don't go too far the other way and be clever at other people's expense. The chapter also gives you some techniques for critical analysis, including tables and diagrams to help you work through the strengths and weaknesses in any scholarly argument, including your own.

Mostly, this chapter is written to enable your dissertation to stand on its own two feet and make a really strong case for the importance and value of your research.

6.1 Who am I to question?

'This lacks analysis' or 'Where is your voice in this?' or 'A bit too descriptive here' or 'What is your position?' These are all examples of feedback that is secretly saying you haven't been critical enough. So, what does your reader want? What does 'being critical' mean anyway? As we will explain, how you see yourself as a scholar translates directly into more scholarly and critical writing. Your reader wants you to behave like a scholar. Let's talk about how you can do that.

The most common sections where students are accused of not being critical enough are literature reviews, research essays, review and synthesis papers, and sometimes discussion sections. All these sections are where you bring together the voices of your scholarly forebears. You have worked to understand said forebears and relay their ideas accurately. You might have identified where they agree and disagree with one another. You may even have identified a thread that weaves through these works and put this forward as the point of view you will adopt. This is what scholars do right? Well, yes, and no.

Being a scholar isn't just about understanding the ideas of other scholars. Scholars must analyse their truth claims. All of them – from a fellow student, right the way through to the greats, the Newton, Darwin and Durkheim of your field. In addition to explaining their ideas, you must also evaluate them, and analyse the validity of the thought process that produced the ideas. While status and celebrity open many doors in life, they should open none when it comes to determining the logic of a knowledge claim. This is what your reader wants of you as a scholar – to weigh and test the claims of others and inevitably find some of them wanting (with the caveat that you sometimes need to do this in a humble way: see Section 6.5 on hedging language later in this chapter).

At this point you might be thinking – consciously or unconsciously: *me – a scholar*? But who am I to question? You may have noticed that you have been accused of being a scholar at several points in this book. We stand by this accusation. While it can feel a little strange to get used to, a scholar is exactly what you are. Get comfortable with this idea. Being a scholar is not about a particular degree, set of post-nominals, or type of employment – it is about a thought process and commitment to the truth (putting aside momentarily all the arguments about what qualifies as 'truth'). From the first class of your first year as a university student, your lecturers and advisors have been trying to teach you what a scholar is and how to be one. In our mind, this makes you a scholar from the very start, albeit a novice one.

The most beautiful thing about being a scholar is that the organisational hierarchy should be perfectly flat when it comes to truth claims (even if in practice it is sometimes not as flat as we would like).[7] Any two scholars are equally entitled to the truth, and the strength of their claims to it lies not in their respective experience or fame, but in the rigour of their argumentation and the quality of their evidence. A problematic claim made by a respected professor retains its problematic nature, and an incisive one made by a novice loses none of its incisiveness.

So, who are you to be critical of the ideas of other scholars? You are their equal! (This is what it means to be a 'peer reviewer' – you are the equal of your reviewers, you are the equal of the people you review.) In realising this, the process of evaluating the claims of others should hopefully not become an agonising addition to your writing, but the most enjoyable part.

How to think (and thus write) in a scholarly way

Adding a more critical dimension to your writing is a more-or-less automatic consequence of cultivating the scholarly mind-set outlined above. Here is a technique that can help you develop scholarly responses to the texts you read and ultimately cite. The technique here relies on developing 'reflexive doubt'.

The trick to 'reflexive doubt' is to train yourself to automatically respond to claims in the texts you read with something like 'I don't believe you – convince me'. Kamler and Thompson (2014) call this the 'hands on hips' stance that puts you on the same level as the other academic writer. Use this stance on yourself as well as others; as you read back your text, imagine yourself as reader saying: 'this is not convincing', or 'how do you know this?'. Then work to convince that imaginary reader!

Using critique tables

You might want to consider using a critique table. A critique table can form part of your note-taking strategy, effectively forcing yourself to evaluate claims fully. A well-crafted critique table is a great writing tool, which gives you all the ammunition you need to explain why the sources you like are worth trusting, and why the ones you dislike are not up to scholarly par.

Critique tables have three columns:

Claim: what does the article say happens? How strongly does it make this claim? (You might want to use verbs, as discussed in Chapter 2, to help you describe the claim.)

Evidence: Does this work reference another scholar, inference from data and provide a warrant, examples, or other kinds of evidence?

Evaluation: This is your bit. How strong is the evidence? Are you convinced? What are the weaknesses or limitations of the evidence? Do these weaknesses destroy the original claim, or are they simply caveats to understanding the claim as stated?

Here is a critique table, taken from Shaun's research (Table 6.1).

Table 6.1 Critique table

Claim	Evidence	Evaluation
Kovac et al. (2009) *tentatively argue that increasing economic power distance between the rich and poor could be the main reason for differences in violent crime rates.*	Cites Smith (2007) who *found a strong correlation* between the Gini-index and violent crime rates globally.	The correlation found by Smith (2007) *is indeed strong*, though the validity of the Gini-index and violent crime measures *could be a problem*. Different countries may report these things differently, which means an apples-with-apples comparison *is not really possible*. This being said, Kovac et al. (2009) made their argument in a speculative fashion, and *this seems appropriate* given the doubts about the consistency of the evidence.

Weave your evaluation into your text to move from descriptive writing to critical writing.

For example (Shaun researched this example before writing it):

> *Descriptive: The main cause of* differences in violent crime rates between countries is the economic power distance between the rich and poor (Kovac et al., 2009). *Therefore,* to reduce violent crime rates, *it is important to* address economic disparity.

The problem with this paragraph is that it takes the authors' claim at face value without much consideration of certainty, and then leaps to a conclusion. Writing like this shows a lack of careful critical evaluation of the claims being used and is red rag to the examiner bulls. Here is the paragraph again, reworked to be more critical:

> *Critical:* Kovac et al. (2009) *put forward the position that* differences in violent crime rates between countries *seem to be well explained by* the economic power distance between the rich and the poor in those countries. *In making this claim,* Kovac et al. *refer to* the statistical work of Smith (2007) which *examined the relationship between the* Gini-index (a measure of economic disparity) and violent crime rates globally. *While it is difficult to be certain that* data gathered on economic disparity and violent crime for different countries will be directly comparable, *the strength of the correlation observed suggests* that there is merit to the Kovac et al. claim of a causal relationship between these factors. *As such, it is worth considering addressing* economic disparity as a means to reduce violence.

While the above is much longer than the first, it is much more transparent about the thought process of the original author. No claims are blindly accepted here. Also, note that this response also goes to the original source that Kovac et al. refer to in order to weigh up its validity. This is important – sometimes you may need to follow chains of evidence several layers deep in order to verify someone's claim.

As we will say again in Chapter 7: critical doesn't mean disagreeing, or even saying why you agree or disagree. Critical goes beyond a kneejerk response by asking significant questions like:

- Why did the researcher write this way?
- Have invisible aspects of the research been assumed and elided from the text?
- How reliable is this analysis?
- What assumptions did the researchers make that might have biased their data?

Finding the answers to these questions doesn't invalidate the original research. Likewise, finding that research was 'biased' or didn't have a big sample doesn't always invalidate the original research either. All research is biased! All research could have a larger sample size, different sampling techniques, more than one location, and so on. Even large sample sizes have limitations. The question isn't 'Was their research perfect?', but 'Was it done well and what is it good for?'. Asking and answering these questions helps you analyse your sources more fully and work out how they speak to – and challenge – your own assumptions.

As you can see, what the reader wants from you is for you to be a reflexively critical scholar, who tests the claims of others for their logic and validity and uses these claims in a manner that is suitable to the task at hand. As a scholar, it is your duty to question the work of others – that is how knowledge advances.

6.2 Can I use 'I'?

If there is one problem we have seen more often than any others it is students worried about using 'I'. Some academics loathe it; others insist students must use it. Some scientists are happy to use it (most biologists), others insist it has no place (especially in disciplines where the passive voice is normal, like physics). Some humanities scholars think using 'I' is morally wrong (most historians) while others believe excising 'I' entirely from your writing is unethical (most sociologists). If the use of the word 'I' had a Facebook relationship status, it would be, 'It's complicated.'

Use of the personal pronoun in academic English is fraught because academia developed a history of prioritising scientific, objective and distancing language, which was then contested. There is no room here to do justice to the complex debate about subjectivity, but a brief history can help us understand the 'I' conundrum better.

In the eighteenth century, the Enlightenment values of objectivity and rationality meant that human observers were increasingly understood to be unreliable. The emerging field of science started to transfer the responsibility for recording the world to inanimate things: instruments and tools. Nonetheless, we do not see the complete removal of the 'I' from scientific texts until the mid-twentieth century. Over this period, it was no longer an 'I' who saw, thought and wrote, but a detached observer who recorded what they saw on the instruments. Hence, we get language like, 'An average of 2km an hour was recorded for these time trials', rather than, say, James Boswell and Samuel Johnson writing in 1785: 'The roof rises in an arch, almost regular, to a height which we could not measure; but I think it about thirty feet' (Johnson and Boswell [1785] 1984, p. 139). Nonetheless, Sword (2012b) has shown that most scientific articles do use 'we' where appropriate, for example, in introducing the hypothesis, but not in describing the methodology. In some disciplines, 'I' or 'we' is replaced with 'the researcher'. In many situations, there is no need to use the 'I' form at all, instead using phrases like: 'This dissertation will argue . . .', 'This experiment will demonstrate . . .', or when using the passive voice (see Chapter 5).

Some Social Science, Arts and Humanities disciplines focus on the inherent subjectivities of what is being observed: small-scale, non-reproducible qualitative studies; creative practices; or literary readings, for example. These studies do not need to be reproduced and are understood to be influenced by the person doing the study. Avoiding the use of 'I' may be seen as erasing your biases and position in the writing, thus intentionally hiding them from the reader. While avoiding the use of 'I', historians make their subjective position clear with strongly subjective verbs and nouns (Sword 2012b) (see further Section 2.5 on verbs). In yet other fields, like Higher Education research, Sword (2012b) found that about half her data sample used personal pronouns and half didn't. So, in practice, the use of 'I' is very much discipline by discipline, university by university, and even academic by academic. Using 'I' is one of the places that students and their teachers, and writers and their editors, often come into conflict.

No matter the style that you finally adopt, splitting out the storyline of your research and an account of your researcher journey is an important part of the editing process (see Chapter 3). We know it was you personally who stayed up till 2 a.m. tending the centrifuge, we know it was you who stood out in the mudflats for hours counting insects. We know you got flu sitting in the air-conditioned archive pouring over incunabula. We know you have RSI from transcribing 100 hours of interview recordings. You know this too, viscerally, in your body. However, you must remove evidence of your visceral experience from the final work. You might want to write about some important detail you learned through doing the research, but these experiences may not belong in the dissertation. Academic readers don't want to know your messy journey; they want a neat map of how to get there themselves, effectively and efficiently. Therefore, carefully and forensically, you must cut yourself out of the draft (perhaps we should say 'your researcher journey needs to be gently placed aside': you can always share extra stuff via a blog, or to your students).

As we keep saying, writing is iterative. What is a good idea for your messy first draft, to get words on the page, is not necessarily a good idea for the text as you submit it to an advisor – or for examination, or for publication. We recommend the following procedure to manage your use of pronouns as you write – and to harness their power appropriately:

First draft: Use 'I' whenever you want

Using 'I' is easy and, if you let yourself do it, will feel natural. Leaving yourself in can help you to write clear active sentences. It helps you define your voice, your position. It helps you say 'Hey! This new original thing? I did that!' or 'This is where I agree with the secondary literature and here's where I don't.' For example:

1 I am going to argue that you should use 'I' in first drafts.
2 I am going to write the first history of wand weevils in Armenian monasteries.

3   I think this is a stupid interpretation of the data.
4   Barry and I filled up 15 pipettes with hydrochloric acid.

Second draft: Go through and take 'I' out of any section that should be focused on your data, sources or case study

You might leave 'I' in for introductions, conclusions and any original analysis. You may also leave it in methods sections – advisedly. Scientists can use the personal pronoun, or the royal 'we' sometimes, to describe what they, as authors, are doing. If your dissertation is by publication, you must explain which parts of the multi-authored papers were your contribution. In a dissertation built from co-authored work, it is correct – in fact, essential – to use 'I' to put yourself back into the text.

Brushing each sentence with objective language is more than a matter of just removing the 'I' of course. You will have to re-parse, sometimes substantially. Look what happens to our four sentences when the subjective 'I' is removed:

1   It is permissible to write 'I' in first drafts according to Mewburn, Firth and Lehmann (2018).
2   This dissertation is the first history of wand weevils in Armenian monasteries.
3   Mewburn's analysis of the data can be disputed.
4   5 pipettes were filled with hydrochloric acid.

The sentences sound 'academic' now, don't they? Number three is definitely passive aggressive, and Barry the lab assistant has disappeared.

If you are using a methodology such as auto-ethnography, or standpoint theory, then you are part of the research and it's going to be difficult and counterproductive to try to avoid using 'I'. In most cases, however, the dissertation is really about medieval kingship, or people using Japanese train stations, or 1930s film. Therefore, the focus should not be on you, the researcher, but on the topic of the research.

Use 'I' when to do otherwise makes the writing clunky and obvious that you are 'writing around' the pronoun. We are not fans of 'one': it's old-fashioned. If you are going to use 'I', do so sparingly. Often the 'I' is implied, in sentences that focus on the data/source/text, for example, academic readers know when you say 'the data suggests' you actually mean, 'I think the data suggests.'

Some replacement phrases are:

- 'this dissertation will argue/demonstrate/suggest;'
- 'the researcher' or 'the research team';
- 'we'.

By your final draft, most of the work should be done

But remember: always use 'I' in the Acknowledgements!

6.3 How not to be unintentionally exclusionary in your writing

For centuries, academic texts claimed to take an 'objective' and scientific position, observing and measuring the world in an unbiased way. Whether they wrote in Latin, French, German or English, these scholars were European, male, straight, and often upper class. This was considered the default setting – and still is.[8] Simone de Beauvoir in *The Second Sex* (1949) demonstrates that even small grammatical choices, such as choice of pronouns ('he' instead of 'she' or 'they'), can continue to impose that view of the world on, and through, our texts.

Even when women, People of Colour, and colonised peoples were actively contributing to the research (and they were), they were not typically included as authors of scholarly works until the middle of the twentieth century (see Wallace 1869; Haraway 1997; Sobel 2017). As a university education has become more widely accessible, and marginalised people have fought for their space at the academic writing table, we have all had to adjust how we write to make sure we include all our potential readers and co-authors. But this is not necessarily difficult. Simply remembering to ask (or Google) what is the current appropriate way to talk about a marginalised group, and being willing to update your writing as appropriate, can be a strong start. We offer this section as three white, straight people who live in Australia, who are committed to being decent allies. Our understanding of this space is developing all the time, so read this with the expectation that you (and we) will have to keep growing.

There are many English words and terms that are tainted by the terrible power games of history. We need to put aside our personal preferences, and call people the name they say they prefer. If a group prefers the term 'First People' over 'Aboriginal', respect their wishes and recognise that preferences can change. You can't get it right for all time, or for all members of an under-represented group. If you make a mistake, the right response is to apologise and change the text accordingly. Keep a watchful eye on leading writers and theorists in these areas. It's your job to educate yourself, not the job of excluded, marginalised or under-represented people to educate you; they have enough work to do overcoming all the extra hurdles that institutions and society put in their way.

At the very least you should aim to be polite, respectful and up to date with the words you use to refer to different groups of people. You can avoid some of the most egregious howlers by writing with these questions in mind:

1 Does the marginalised person get to be a full human, with an identity that is more than the minority group they are associated with?

2 Do the majority of that group request this form of address?

3 Has the term been widely used in the contemporary academic literature within the last five years?

4 If you are not a member of the group in question, is the language you are using approved for outsiders? Some marginalised groups have reclaimed

terms formally used to denigrate their people to empower themselves. Examples of reclaiming terms include disability activists who use hashtags like #CriptheVote; Alison Bechdel's series 'Dykes to Watch Out For'; Sarah Ahmed's writing about 'the queer'; Jay Z and Kanye West's 'Niggas in Paris'. At the same time, don't censor in-groups who reclaim offensive or potentially offensive terms. Quote them accurately – but don't use these terms yourself!

5 Do you assume a group is homogeneous, or do you recognise variation among individuals? Do you position exceptions to your prejudice as exceptions – or do you acknowledge that every group in society is made up of a mix of people?

6 Have you read in the group's field as thoughtfully as you have in the other fields? Have you acknowledged the academic work done by members of that group?

7 Are you 'speaking for' a group? What authority do you have for that?

8 Are you speaking to others who claim to be 'speaking for' a group? What authority do they have? Is anyone missing from the conversation?

9 What are you assuming about that group? Are you claiming this with rigorous statistics, or assuming this is something everyone knows? Do we actually all know it, or are you making racist/sexist/ableist/etc. assumptions?

The list above is just the basics of respectful writing. You don't get a prize for doing everything on this list, but you do get demerit points if you can't even be bothered with these basics. You can – and should – go further. Here are some ways to do just that.

Gender

Sexism is deeply ingrained in the English language, but we should resist it. As a start, never use 'he' as default. It is acceptable to use 'they' or 's/he' or 'he or she' interchangeably. Increasingly, academic writers are avoiding 'she or he' as it assumes everyone is male or female – treating gender as fixed or binary – when there are as many people who are intersex as there are redheads. The singular 'they' was common in English until the eighteenth century, when linguists invented rules to make English more like Latin. In the twenty-first century the singular 'they' has been widely recommended by linguists (Swift and Miller 1995) and our own publisher's guidelines!

Check your hypothetical examples and anonymised case studies. Unless there is a good reason, you should aim for 50 per cent male and female names. Check you aren't ascribing mostly female names to emotional or family examples, or examples where things go wrong. Likewise make sure you don't use mostly male names to describe logical, science and work examples, or examples where the participant succeeded.

Gender bias can go deeper than just the words you use. For example, experimental research has used the male body as default. Medical research carried out on male, but not female, mice, might mean you miss critical differences caused by different body chemistry. Being inclusive in your research design is also essential.

LGBT, LGBTIQ, LGBT+

At the moment, the acronym for people who do not identify as cisgendered and heterosexual is LBGTIQ+.[9] However, this is an area where conversations and norms are developing fast, so stay tuned. Also, LGBTIQ+ is generally used for the broad rainbow coalition of non-heterosexual people; whereas some research focuses specifically on an aspect of sexuality or gender experience, for example same-sex attracted men, or transgendered women. Be careful to understand the specifics of how to write about the experiences of diverse groups of people. For example, 'Queer' is an in-group term with a subtle and shifting range of meanings, and should only be used by outsiders when referencing Queer Theory. As we mentioned above, be particularly careful about using the correct pronoun to refer to transgender, intersex and non-binary individuals.

If you have ambitions to be an excellent academic writer, you must work to avoid bias, which includes understanding variations of sexuality and gender identity. Most universities have courses where you can learn about the whole spectrum of human gender identity and sexual preferences. If you did not come from a country which routinely talks about these differences, you might have to do some confronting and challenging work.

Race

The two big issues with writing about race and nationalities are: racial stereotyping and racial othering. Remembering that people are individual humans will avoid this issue. This is why, in academic writing, we avoid the shorthand forms 'the Chinese' or 'the French', which are often used in journalism. Instead use 'the French government', or 'students with a French background'. Never use 'the' before a race term, e.g. 'the African-Americans' or 'the Swedish'. Using 'the' implies there is a definite and singular group (implying they are all the same, which no serious researcher could assume).

Ways to talk about race have changed significantly over the last century. For example, in the 1920s, African-American members of the Harlem Renaissance in the US talked about themselves as 'the Negro' as a positive term. In the 1970s, African-Americans used terms like 'Blaxploitation', and 'Black Power'. Now 'black' is mostly used as an in-group term (for example, 'Black Lives Matter'). When outsiders talk about this group, terms like 'African-American' or the wider coalition of 'People of Colour' is more acceptable in the United States. In the UK, on the other hand, the same group are officially described as belonging to the 'Black and Ethnic Minority' group, who may have African, Afro-Caribbean, or African-American heritage. In Australia, people of African descent are often called 'ethnic minorities'. 'Black' tends to be used by Indigenous people to talk about themselves (as in the titles *Dark Emu, Black Seeds,* or *Black Swan*). Non-Indigenous Australians should use terms like 'Indigenous', or 'Aboriginal and Torres Strait Islander' or 'First Nations' people (always with capital letters). It's complicated, we know, but what isn't complicated when it comes to race and power?

Colonialism

Our observations about language around race need to be considered within the broader movement towards 'de-colonising research' (Tuhiwai Smith 1999; Nakata 2007). This research has highlighted that we should not assume the academic is the person who 'really understands what's happening', instead of valuing the knowledge of the person who lives the experience every day. In the same vein, we need to be alert to the tendency to value only some voices from a group as 'authentic', which silences other members of that group. Can an urban, middle-class Indigenous person speak for the people in the Islands, to use the example given by Nakata (2007), is their input still valid?

Even when not writing explicitly about colonised peoples, it is important to remember the ways in which colonialism enables many aspects of research: from museum collections, to national parks, to oceans, to the land where our universities are built and the natural resources that boosted our local and empire economies. Many of the founding fathers of our disciplines (Charles Darwin, Adam Smith, Plato) benefitted from colonising power to support their research. So, thinking about how we got to be lucky enough to get access to our research materials, and who we cite about our research, is important for all of us.

Disability

Are you being ableist? By which we mean, do you assume that 'normal' is a body that conforms to those famous etchings by Leonardo Da Vinci – healthy, muscular and fit? Terms in academic writing books are frequently ableist: like talking about 'binge vs snack writing'; suggesting your writing is 'flabby'; or talking about 'limping onwards' to the writing deadline. In academic writing, we might describe ourselves as being 'blind' to certain outcomes, or for policy to 'fall on deaf ears' of governments. Such language is ableist. It's not okay to use a negative and dismissive term about people's bodies as a metaphor for things we disapprove of, or do not like.

Class

Just like race and gender identity, you need to be alert to class bias. Do you unconsciously equate poverty or unemployment with moral failing; or do you use 'bourgeois' or 'upper-class' in a pejorative way? Our research and analysis will be weaker if we allow unfounded biases to keep us from understanding the complex lives of the people we study. Our whole research community will be weaker if we allow those biases to exclude readers and researchers from our academic writing.

As we have pointed out many times in this book, though – there is one aspect of class that is important to include in academic writing. In English-speaking countries, being 'middle class' or 'professional-managerial class' is often associated with a university education, a professional job, and a standard accent. In other words, you need to sound middle class to sound like you belong at university. The rules of middle-class language are so intrinsic to academic writing that not to speak like a reserved middle-class white person is not to 'speak academic'. While we show you how to conform with these (largely unspoken) language rules to help you succeed academically, our message to conform should not be conflated with implicit approval. We found ourselves deeply conflicted at times writing this book, but we decided it was important to help you understand how and why certain kinds of language are expected.

Finally

On the one hand, knowledge is power. When you know the hidden rules and underlying assumptions of language, you are in a better position to challenge dominant modes of language use, and to adopt other modes if you wish. Mostly, though, we encourage you to think about being kind and respecting other people's lived experiences, rather than rigidly holding on to our (often outdated) ideas about grammatical purity.

6.4 Avoiding excessive cleverness

Inger's PhD advisor once described her work as 'flippant' – what a classic academic burn! Has this happened to you? Academia is a serious business. Sometimes you can be criticised if you are seen to be having too much fun in your writing, especially if the reader is not laughing along. Symptoms of too much fun include in-jokes, excessive cleverness, archness, or a snide tone. While we are trying to keep this an interdisciplinary book, this section will probably resonate most with scholars in the humanities, where there is a history of such writing. Postmodern theory writing in the 1990s and early 2000s suffered from excessive cleverness. Coincidentally, this period was when many of your academic advisors were doing their PhD training, which is why cleverness is now about as fashionable as most academics' outfits (ahem, snide joke). In this section, we discuss how important it is to meet the reader where they are, and provide text that is straightforward and scholarly, rather than something that belongs in a student newspaper.

People who write doctoral theses are clever. They think about things deeply and tend to work in a narrow field for a long time. As a consequence, academics build up a lexicon of in-group words and phrases that are meaningful to them but meaningless to outsiders. This language has several names: jargon, technical terms, buzzwords. As academics dwell in their scholarly worlds, they get to know other scholars well. They meet up regularly at conferences, read each other's work, and follow each other's public lectures, Twitter rants and articles for The Conversation, the *Times Literary Supplement* or *National Geographic*. When academics are together in person, or hanging out on social media or the email circular (do listservs still exist?), it is socially acceptable to make in-jokes about quarks or p numbers or Žižek or Reviewer 2. Most of your academic colleagues warmly respond to your puns and jokey references. When you make clever jokes in your lectures, presentations, and conversations, people laugh. They might even clap. Awesome. (We all know this is true. People laugh at our jokes, they clap in our presentations – and it makes us feel wonderful.) All these situations we have described are crucial to creating academic identities through making 'in-groups' and 'out-groups'. Knowing enough about the group and its rules, and being able to deploy them correctly, being able to twist them enough to be a joke, demonstrates you belong. The more approval you receive, the deeper your sense of belonging will be (there is extensive academic research about this, which we won't go into here for reasons of space, but trust us that it exists).

Much of academic life is boring and lonely, so telling jokes to others, and to yourself, as a way of enlivening your writing and research, can be very much appreciated, in the right settings. A dissertation is not one of those settings.[10] Everybody understands what it's like when you stay up to 2 a.m. on too much coffee and Gummi bears (and perhaps have been reading too many articles published in 1998), when you think it's a brilliant idea to entitle a chapter '(Re-) presentation of our bodies, our (s)elves in online spaces: feminist trolls and dysphoria/diaspora identities', or 'The fourth be with you: hands solo driving off-road'. We might even like it if you used it in a group setting, like a symposium or on social media. However, everyone would be really grateful if, in your dissertation, you could just call it 'Female magic creatures disagreeing in online beauty forums in North America and Southeast Asia', or 'A new mechanism for safer one-handed steering in four-wheel drive vehicles', or whatever it is that you actually mean to say.

In a dissertation, you must demonstrate your qualifications to join the ranks of academic peers through your sober, diligent hard work. You must painstakingly demonstrate you have done the research labour with enough care and precision. You must prove you can be trusted to teach younger researchers, apply for grants, review other scholars' writing, and publish. When you graduate, you will be expected to be a mentor to new researchers, or you may lead a research team, or manage academic staff. To qualify for these privileges, you need to demonstrate your competence as a scholarly researcher and writer. This prerequisite is one of the reasons that doctoral theses are often quite dull, awkward texts. Yes, you do have to put in all of your workings. Yes, your examiner does want to read a literature review and methodology, even though these will almost always be cut out before publication. A lot – perhaps most – of your dissertation will not be sparkly, exciting, peppy bits of writing, but that is the genre and you must conform (for now).

In this way, doing a dissertation is a bit like a driving test. The purpose of the test is to show you are qualified to drive on your own, take passengers who can't drive and manage a tonne of steel at 100km/hr with other traffic. When you are doing your driving test, you don't show off your ability to do 'dough-nuts', or any other racing driver tricks. You hold the steering wheel at 'two and ten' and ostentatiously turn on the indicator at least three seconds before you turn a corner. During a driving test, you are being watched, so you can't just glance into your mirrors like you would years later; you slowly and obviously turn your head, so the examiner can see you do it. This might not be how you will drive in real life, but it's how you must drive to pass the test because your examiner is not psychic and has no other basis to trust you. Your driving exam-iner has not followed you around your suburb, or hung out in the back of your car for weeks (thank goodness!). They sit next to you for less than an hour, watch you and make a decision on your readiness to go out on your own. So, don't be the clever clogs who doesn't look like they are taking this seriously, be the sensible, careful driver you know you ought to be, even if just for the test.

How do you demonstrate your sober judgement in your writing? First of all, don't think about looking clever, think about your academic reader. Academic readers often read dissertations on the weekend, on planes, or in the evening. On the one hand, this means they have an extended and uninterrupted opportu-nity to read your work. On the other, it means they are giving up time they could be resting, sleeping, socialising or watching movies. Your academic examiner is less rested because they are doing the public service of reading your dissertation, so be gentle with them. Help them focus on the important things like:

- Have you sustained an argument all the way through your literature review?
- Did you do enough research?
- Was the research rigorous enough?
- Did you justify your original contribution?

If they have to decode a whole load of humour too, you are just making the task of reading more exhausting.

We are not saying make your writing boring, repetitive and turgid. Keep it clear, straightforward, explicit and sequential, so your reader only has to read it once, not multiple times to try to understand what you are trying to say (see way back in Chapter 2 where we discussed vagueness). Flowery, archaic, oblique and self-referential writing is not good, because it focuses on the writing itself. Clear, straightforward, explicit and sequential writing focuses on the research, knowledge and ideas you are trying to convey. Look out for the moments where your tone starts to stray into emotional territory. Focus on expanding your point with rigorous evidence, or academic language.

The forms of cleverness we are objecting to here all use a tone of superiority. This kind of language is all about you looking good and can also be used to exclude or diminish others. Be especially careful of excessive cleverness in your literature section. Yes, you have to apply critique, but don't be a jerk. Other scholars may be wrong sometimes, but they needn't be made to look stupid. Other researchers may disagree with you, but they needn't be made to look inferior. You can make your point assertively, respectfully and collegially. If you don't do critique in a generous way, you are sure to look like an amateur, not the life of the party.

For future reference, here are the signs of cleverness that you should try to avoid, and how to achieve the same effect with scholarly language:

In-jokes: evidence of belonging and knowing the language. Instead: use jargon correctly, use citations to show you are in the field.

Excessive cleverness: evidence of being too smart for a dissertation. Instead: think about what you can do to make the dissertation ready for publication.

Archness (a tone of superior mischief): evidence that you know more than others. Instead: demonstrate your expertise in the area through your data and analysis. Confidently state your original contribution to knowledge.

Snide tone: evidence that you think others are wrong. Instead: straightforwardly set out your disagreement, or use phrases like 'while X has argued, more recent scholarship suggests . . .'

6.5 Hedging and boosting language

While academic writers need to take a position in their writing, they must be careful not to over-claim, especially when putting forward a theory to explain the observed evidence. Skilful academic writers know exactly how to employ 'hedging language' (e.g. might, maybe, sometimes, perhaps). Knowing how to write in a way that your reader understands your level of certainty is fundamental to being an academic, especially in the sciences. In this section, we discuss how to write about uncertainty.

Being precise is one of the most, if not the most, important of the academic values. We must be as precise about our uncertainty as we are about everything else. Hedging language is tentative. These terms help us modify strong claims without losing valuable nuance.

Sometimes we see writing advice that suggests writers get rid of hedging language to avoid sounding 'wishy-washy', but remember – when it comes to writing you are at a passive-aggressively competitive middle-class dinner party. Do not conflate 'taking a stand' with 'writing forcefully'. Just as yelling louder doesn't help you win a fight with your family member at a Sunday dinner, getting rid of hedging language to look more confident does not endear you to your academic reader.

People not trained in academic ways of thinking can find hedging language extremely frustrating to read. However, we are dealing with hard-core notions of truth and certainty here – we must, therefore, be careful how we make our knowledge claims. With the possible exception of maths proofs, all research is, to some extent, tentative. Hedging language introduces intentional vagueness to avoid sending clear signals to your reader.

You might be thinking: 'but early in this book you told me I should avoid vagueness and now you are telling me to introduce it deliberately? What gives?!'. We know it sounds contradictory, but when you write scholarly text, you must bear in mind that you are communicating within academia, not just communicating about what you found out. Going with the idea that academic writing is a form of fencing or a dinner party, there are (mostly hidden) rules around how you can express interpretations of data (see Chapter 2). Hedging language helps indicate the precise degree of uncertainty you feel about a finding, fact or idea.

In its most straightforward form, hedging terms are used to avoid overstating claims. Even where the evidence points to a highly likely conclusion, there is usually some degree of doubt, so use a hedging word somewhere in the sentence. For example:

> Using chlorine on wands *may* reduce the prevalence of wand weevils.
> or
> From the data, *it is likely that* adding red stripes makes Quidditch gowns more aerodynamic.

These sentences leave room for further research (by you or by another researcher) which may come to slightly stronger conclusions.

At the next level of hedging, intentionally vague language is used to force the reader to 'read between the lines' about what the writer thinks. For example:

> *One possible reason for* frequent wand weevil infestation is excessive use of Dr Snape's Sectumsempra curse during routine maintenance.

Does the writer really believe that the Sectumsempra curse is the problem here? We are not sure. This technique is useful if we want to, as Hyland (1998) puts it: 'seek self-protection from negative consequences of poor judgment'. For example, imagine you have been taking photos of the night sky each night and noticed extra stars in one image. You could form a theory that the extra stars are UFOs, and write:

> The extra stars shown in the table and images above are UFOs.
> Well, that's one theory anyway.

It's highly likely that an academic reader would just put a line through this sentence and write, 'Rubbish!'. Instead, you could surround your claim with a bit of sophisticated hedging, like so:

> *One possible interpretation of the data* shown in the tables and images above is the existence of UFOs *or another, unexpected stellar artefact.*

This sentence is top notch hedging in action. We have left the reader unsure of whether we believe the statement by including a classic hedge word ('possible') at the start of the sentence and then throwing in a modifier ('or') at the end.

In our UFO example, hedging language functions to distance ourselves from the proposition about alien life, so we don't entirely 'own it'. It's a bit like putting something on the table, backing away, then pointing at the item and asking the reader what they think it is, rather than telling them what you believe it is.

The use of hedging language is connected to how we make knowledge within communities. We use hedging to signal to the reader that we are cautious, careful researchers who pay due attention to the accepted ideas and theories in our field, not cranks. Cultivating the right degree of academic humility is a matter of careful word choice, including careful use of hedges. This is one of the many reasons academic writing is accused of being abstruse, but it's unavoidable when you are a student and need someone to approve of your work.

Academia is profoundly hierarchical, and it is important to bear this in mind when you want to disagree with anyone else's theories, interpretations or evidence. Hedging can help us when we need to 'soften' a sentence that can sound abrupt and rude without it; the secret here is to have just enough padding to be respectful without getting waffle-y (see Section 5.6 on filler words). You will often disagree with another researcher's findings, but you can't just come out and say, 'Smith is wrong to claim . . .'. After all, you are going to meet each other at conferences for the next 20 years. The correct tone is middle-class and passive-aggressive, remember? How about: 'It has been claimed by scholars including Chang (1986) and Lorenzo (1992) that Smith's claim is overstated.' That's probably about right.

Academics can also use the opposite of hedging language; what Hyland calls 'boosters'. Boosters are words like 'clearly', 'obviously', 'indeed', 'undoubtedly', 'in fact, 'actually' and 'of course'. These words and statements show increased certainty and confidence, even enthusiasm. Boosters are used to draw people into sharing your point of view. (We are clearly fans: the original draft of this book contained a lot of boosters, which we toned down in subsequent edits.) Boosters are also used to anticipate a reader's reaction to a statement, for instance:

> *Of course*, the use of the Sectumsempra curse is routine in most instances of wood weevil infestation, but we *certainly* should question whether curses are the best method of weevil removal.

In this sentence, the writer implies that 'everyone knows' about the role of the Sectumsempra curse, thus signalling membership of a knowledge community. Most of the time, you will only be using boosters as back-handed hedging statements, as this example does.[11]

We encourage you to start developing an 'eye' for hedges and add them to your writing toolkit. Hedges help us indicate the precise degree of uncertainty we feel about a finding, fact or idea. They strengthen or weaken the force of statements, express deference to, or membership of, your academic tribe. This section has covered truly the next level of academic writing, so be patient.

Look for hedging language in other people's writing and attempt to emulate it. The Manchester Phrase bank has a useful list of hedging phrases that can be adapted to all your intentional vagueness needs.

Use hedging phrases to signal distance from a position

Here are some of our favourite phrases to signal that you are distancing your-self from common positions in your discipline:

It is thought that . . .
It is believed that . . .
It has been reported that . . .
It is a widely held view that . . .
It has commonly been assumed that . . .

You can also use the hedging phrases to avoid over-generalisation

Compare the choice of words in Tables 6.2 and 6.3.

Table 6.2 Hedging phrases example 1

Ozone levels	often	exceed WHO levels in many cities.
	generally	
	frequently	
	sometimes	
	occasionally	
	nearly always	

Table 6.3 Hedging phrases example 2

Ozone is toxic to	most	living organisms.
	almost all	
	some types of	
	many types of	
	the majority of	
	certain types of	

6.6 Argument diagramming

Learning to argue like an academic is a skill you start developing during under-graduate study and continue to refine through all levels, right up to the PhD. Developing academic arguments is one of the most subtle and challenging parts of the research degree learning process. Formal logic teaching is central to the European, UK and North American academic systems, but less common in other places, like Australia. Even if you have had formal training, it can be hard to translate the concepts into prose. Weak or poorly joined-up arguments tend to generate the most frustratingly vague feedback from academics. If you are getting comments like 'I'm not sure what you mean here', 'this seems irrelevant' or 'get to the point', your reader is probably not convinced by the logic of your argument.

Since we don't have time to rehash a 3-year undergraduate degree in the Cambridge model, or even time for a semester of North American Comp/Rhet101, let's look at one quick way to get the gist of your argument by using argument diagrams. You can use diagrams to construct arguments for any paper or chapter – either in advance of trying to make the argument as a guide to writing, or later, to diagnose where your argument might be weak. The thread, gaps or disjoints of your argument can be hard to see when you are working with paragraphs; the words tend to get in the way. Drawing your logic as a diagram is a quick and easy way to see whether the argument 'hangs together'.

The method outlined here is from *The Palgrave Handbook of Critical Thinking in Higher Education* (van Gelder 2015), based on the work of Munro Beardsley (1950). Inger made some modifications to the method and tested it on both science and humanities students. She found it translates across disci-

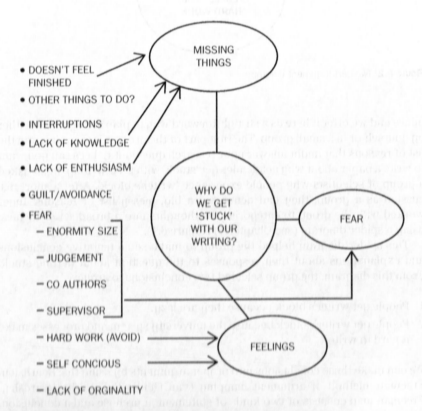

Figure 6.1 Example argument spider diagram

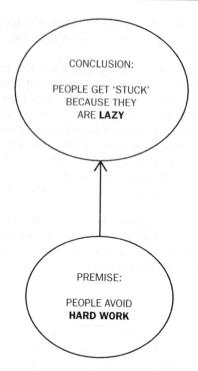

Figure 6.2 Two-part argument diagram

plines and we offer it here as a straightforward way to plan an argument, either by yourself or in a small group. The first part of the process is to brainstorm the list of reasons that might answer your research question(s). Let's say you want to write a paper about why academics get 'stuck' with their writing. Inger asked a group of scientists why people experience 'writer's block'. After a short discussion as a group, they had generated a big, messy list of reasons. Inger worked with the group to categorise the thoughts into a broad set of themes, using a spider diagram (see Chapter 4) (Figure 6.1).

This spider diagram helped the group to make some tentative conclusions and explanations about their responses to the question about getting stuck. From this diagram, the group selected two conclusions to argue:

1 People get writer's block because they are lazy.
2 People get writer's block because the university system and processes make it hard to write.

We can make these conclusions into proper arguments by using the 'Beardsley-Freeman' method of argument mapping (van Gelder 2015). The Beardsley-Freeman map consists of two kinds of statement: a premise and a conclusion. A premise is simply a proposition or 'truth statement' that supports a conclusion.

You can have many premises and conclusions – the argument bit comes in how you arrange them.

The simplest form of argument is premise -> conclusion. You can draw it with lines and bubbles, as shown in Figure 6.2.

The beauty of a diagram is the thinking becomes embodied in the drawing and can be used as a visual aid to writing:

> People who are lazy avoid hard work. Laziness leads to people getting stuck in their writing

Sounds a bit . . . thin, doesn't it? The diagram is as simple as the sentences; there just isn't much meat on those argument bones. We could try to beef it up with a convergent diagram: more than one premise leading to a conclusion. To do this we need a more complex argument diagram with two forks leading to the conclusion (Figure 6.3).

We can translate this diagram into a sentence or two:

> People avoid hard work. Avoiding work can make them feel guilty. Guilt and laziness lead to people getting stuck.

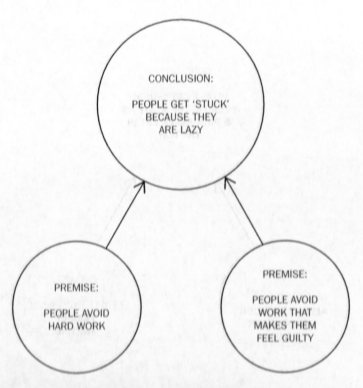

Figure 6.3 The argument diagram now has two premises

When we try to make the simple argument into a more complex one, the fundamental flaws in logic start to become apparent. What we have here are simply three statements that are not linked in a logical progression. Simply stringing them together does not convince because there are gaps: How do these things lead to one another? Are they actually related? Nothing on our list will provide the bridge. We need more complexity to build a satisfying, robust and therefore convincing argument.

Let's start with the other conclusion: 'People get stuck with their writing because the university system and processes make it hard to write.' Starting with a convergent diagram (more than one premise pointing to a conclusion), we could come up with something like that shown in Figure 6.4.
We could translate this diagram into text:

> Academics work in massive bureaucracies where there is a lot of 'other' work to do in addition to writing. In addition to this time constraint, some academics fear writing. It is easy to see how people can get 'stuck': systems and processes get in the way.

It's a much more complex argument, but it's not yet convincing. Neither premise, on its own, logically connects to the conclusion. There are a couple

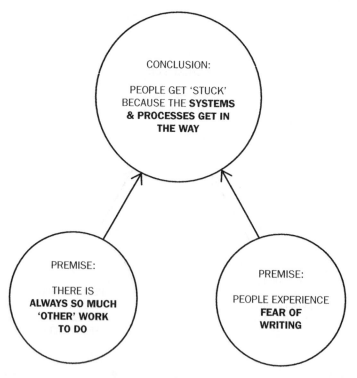

Figure 6.4 Alternative hypothesis argument diagram

more argument diagrams we can try. For example, we could build a serial arrangement: one premise leads to another premise and then the conclusion. Tackling the left-hand side of Figure 6.4, we could supplement it with a serial argument map with another item off the original brainstorming list, like that in Figure 6.5.

An additional premise between the original premise and conclusion fills in a gap and makes for a much richer string of ideas. We could render this diagram into text:

> Academics work in massive bureaucracies where there is a lot of 'other' work to do in addition to writing. It's highly likely that people who sit down to write will be interrupted and lose a sense of 'flow'. Researchers have claimed that a 'flow state' is critical to the creative process. If people are always being interrupted, it's very hard for them to bring all their creative energies to their writing, which leads to people getting stuck.

We could then look at the other side of our convergent argument diagram where we look at how fear might contribute to being stuck. We could use a

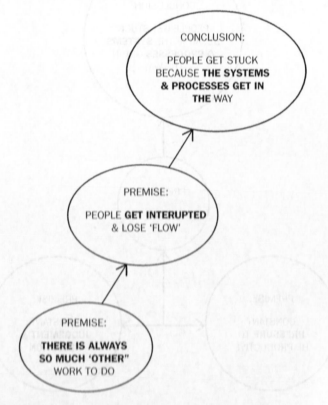

Figure 6.5 Spider diagram with alternative hypothesis developed through serial argument map

linked argument map to make this premise more valid. A linked argument is when one premise depends on another to be valid (Figure 6.6).

We could render this diagram into sentences:

> In the contemporary academy there is constant pressure on academics to be productive, yet the standard that is imposed is never lowered to compensate for the extra demands. It's no wonder that people develop 'performance anxiety': a fear that they can't produce enough writing in the time allowed, which leads to a feeling of being stuck.

We are nearly there. When you have a satisfyingly complex diagram, the thinking has been done and can serve as a handy prop for academic writing.

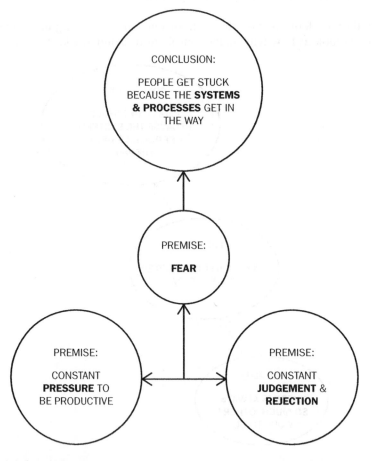

Figure 6.6 Completing the alternative hypothesis, mapped though spider diagrams, with linked argument map

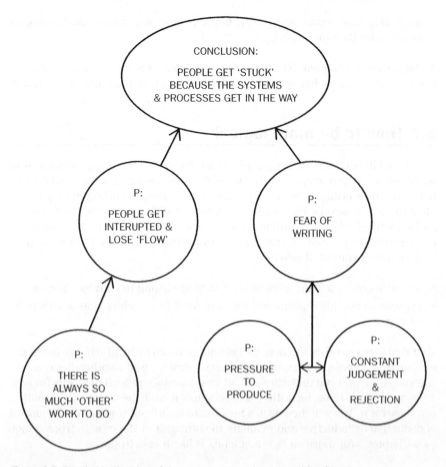

Figure 6.7 Bringing both sides of the argument together in a spider diagram

Let's put the two sides of the argument back together in one diagram (Figure 6.7).

Using Figure 6.7, Inger was able to quickly write this paragraph:

The nature of the university systems and processes slows down or even stops people writing. In a vast, complex bureaucracy like a university, there is always a constant stream of 'other' work an academic must do. This work imposes a series of deadlines and therefore has the potential to lead to constant interruptions of writing – a factor known to slow down writing productivity. Universities are subject to broader systems pressures, like ranking tables which put demands on academics to be continuously productive – subjecting their articles to peer review which can be stressful and demoralising. Conventional journals cannot absorb the extra papers and articles, leading to a constant stream of rejections. Under these circumstances, it is hardly surprising that some academics develop fear and avoidance behaviours which stifle their productivity.

A diagrammed argument like this is ready to have references, data, and other evidence added, and then it can be added to your draft. So, if in doubt, draw it!

6.7 How to be more logical

As we said in Section 6.6, many students have not been formally taught how to make academic arguments. As the basis of every good argument is solid logic, your ability to critique the arguments of others hinges on how well you can identify logical inconsistencies. By knowing the difference between deductive and inductive logic, and learning a simple procedure to evaluate them, you will be in a stronger position to critique the arguments of others in your writing.

Arguments consist of two parts:

- a conclusion or a main point of view they are trying to convince you of;
- reasons (also called premises) that are used to convince you of this point of view.

Your first step is to identify these two elements. It can be helpful to use highlighters for this; choose one colour for the conclusion, and another for reasons. Alternatively, you can underline, circle, or do anything else that works for you, as long as you have identified the conclusion and the reasons the author provides for it. You will then be in a position to figure out whether the argument is deductive or inductive and evaluate the strength of the case in front of you (see Chapter 2 for more on how academia is like a courtroom).

Deduction

Deductive reasoning goes top down. We know certain big-picture things are true, so we can assume subordinate things are true.

A deductive argument is one where the writer is implying that if the reasons are all correct, the conclusion must be correct. In other words, they are stating their argument with perfect certainty. Here's an example (note that conclusions can come at the beginning or end of an argument):

All cars get wet in the rain *[law]*.

It has rained *[reason]*,

so the car is wet *[conclusion]*.

When an argument like this is made, you have multiple angles of attack when it comes to offering a critique.

First, ask whether the reasons they have offered are sufficient for the conclusion – have they left anything out? It isn't uncommon for writers to suppress reasons, either because they think they are common sense, or because they hope you won't notice. In the example above, the below is a suppressed reason:

> To get wet from rain, a car needs to be outside.

Next, we need to ask if all of the reasons are really true. In this case, the suppressed reason is true. As a result, the whole argument becomes questionable. A completely certain argument has a fundamental weakness; if any reason is of questionable truth, the whole argument becomes problematic.

However, some deductive reasoning is required in a dissertation. It's okay to accept gravity or intersectionality as valid and move forward.

Deductive arguments do sound very certain. If you happen to make a deductive argument where the conclusion is not guaranteed based on the reasons, must you do away with it? Not necessarily. First, you could use hand-wavy hedging techniques from earlier in this chapter:

> *Often*, if it rains, the car will get wet.

This may be a situation where a hedging term is avoiding proper research. If you see an argument like this, you can still critique it; you just do so based on whether you think they have over- or under-stated the probability of the claim they are making.

Better, we could use an inductive logic technique.

Induction

Induction starts from evidence and then tries to make generalizable claims. Unlike a deductive argument, an inductive argument has the intention of being probabilistic about its conclusion.

Let's revisit the above argument. In this version, we have taken care to include our previously hidden reason and some hedging language:

> If it rains and the car is outside, it is likely that it will get wet. It has rained, so the car is probably wet.

As you can see, it is much harder to disprove this argument. However, we might quibble over whether 'probably' means 50 per cent or 80 per cent likelihood.

Putting it all together

By understanding the above, you have some of the basic machinery you need to be more critical of the arguments of others, and to build logical arguments for yourself.

Here's a useful procedure:

1 Identify the conclusion and reasons of the argument you are examining.
2 Are all of the reasons that are needed for the argument present?
   (a) If no, you can critique the argument for failing to include all of the necessary reasons.
3 Does it seem likely that all of the reasons are true?
   (a) If no, you can critique the argument for being based on poor reasons, or for being too absolute in its handling of them.
4 At this point, the argument seems to be in good shape. You can offer a positive critique by saying that the argument's reasons are acceptable, and the conclusion seems reasonable based on these. Or alternatively, if you are writing an argument, this means that you have done your best to bolster it against criticism.

Let's take a more realistic example argument and apply this procedure to it:

> Increases in rates of the common cold in winter time are not directly caused by increased exposure to cold weather *[conclusion]*. What we call the common cold, is actually a set of symptoms caused by infection with one of a number of viruses *[reason]*. Further, viruses are usually caught from other people and not from the environment *[reason]*. In cold weather, people tend to spend more time indoors in greater proximity to one another *[reason]*, and this leads to an increase in transmission of the viruses causing colds *[reason]*.

1 Where is the conclusion and what are its reasons? You'll note that the conclusion actually turns up in the beginning. This isn't all that rare, and can be useful for readers to identify the main point.
2 Are all the reasons we need actually present? In this case, it seems that we don't need any extra reasons to support our conclusion.
3 Here's where things might get interesting – we can doubt whether the reasons have been demonstrated to be true. While it is true that people spend more time indoors in winter time, a quick Google search will reveal that it is not well established that this leads to increases in rates of the common cold. If we are critiquing the argument, here is our angle of attack. Alternatively, if we are making this argument, we might switch to a hedging approach:

> Increases in rates of the common cold in winter time *might not be* caused by increased exposure to cold weather *[conclusion]*. What we call the common cold, is actually a set of symptoms caused by infection with one of a number of viruses *[reason]*. Further, viruses are *usually* caught from other people and not from the environment *[reason]*. In cold weather, people *tend to* spend more time indoors in greater proximity to one another *[reason]*, and *this could lead to* an increase in transmission of the viruses causing colds *[reason]*.

See how the specific words make all the difference here? The argument now survives to the next step.

4   Much the best way to test an argument is to go and gather more data! Inductive logic doesn't start from other people's propositions, but from raw information, so being a researcher gives you the tools to test other people's claims, and to make your own.

If you find this process useful and would like to understand it more formally, it might be a good idea to get your hands on a good book on basic propositional logic – don't let its somewhat mathematical presentation scare you. Otherwise, a basic introduction to Ancient Greek syllogisms will help. Once you master the basics of logic, it can be a potent tool in helping you evaluate and write arguments.

7 'Where's your discussion section?': structuring your work as a whole

The structure of your dissertation is critical to helping readers understand your work and ideas. The kinds of chapters you include, and the order you put them in, should follow a logical arrangement that helps make your overall argument. You might be able to follow a standard outline, or you might need to put more thought into the structure. You may also need to defend your decision to examiners and readers used to a particular way of doing things.

In this chapter, we discuss relations between form and function in a book-length dissertation, and other long forms of academic writing, such as a minor thesis. These days, there are many kinds of dissertations, from the conventional 'big book' to collections of published papers and creative works. This variety means you must exercise your academic judgement about the type of chapters and sections you need. Understanding the different ways to structure your dissertation helps you to make decisions about what to include and exclude.

In this chapter, we also turn our attention to the sections that cause most academic writing troubles for students: the literature review, glossary and abstract, which require specialised techniques. We include some tools for taking notes that will help you synthesise the various parts of your writing. Final drafts of these sections should only be attempted when your dissertation is close to being submitted; our advice is designed to make these final jobs much easier.

Finally, this section encourages you to dwell on your readers' experience. Different readers may take different paths through your document. Examiners often read a dissertation out of order, so the structure must give them a fluid reading journey, even if they start with the bibliography and conclusion. To this end, we show you how to have a radically different chapter or section and make it look like a feature, not a weird addition. The reader should also leave the dissertation with the feeling that you knew what you were doing, even if they didn't like it!

Considering the dissertation as a whole work encourages you to step back and look at the big picture – which can be both exciting and scary. As always, we talk about our own experiences and struggles with getting writing done and show how to get to the end of this writing marathon!

7.1 Designing your dissertation as a whole work

'This piece needs a complete re-structure!'. No student writer wants this feedback because it means work, lots of work. Restructuring an essay is painful enough, but that pain is magnified when you are writing anything resembling a book. During the writing process, you deal with individual parts in isolation. You dive deep into the literature for your literature review or spend hours on finessing tables for results. You might be focusing on a particular case study, or a group of related events, a short period, or working on specific examples.

The number and variety of pieces you have to put together add more complexity. These days, dissertations can include journal articles published elsewhere; or practice-based research artefacts (usually creative works). Each of these projects is a significant research undertaking on their own, representing months of work. As a result of all this fragmented research and writing, you can end up with various discrete parts that may or may not relate to each other.

The dissertation genre offers you some templates for putting together the various parts. These are like containers for information.

- The most conventional is the 'IMRAD' format: introduction, method, results and discussion. IMRAD is most common in STEM (science, technology, engineering and maths). IMRAD is sometimes seen as the 'right' way to structure a dissertation and is certainly the most acceptable format if you are undertaking experimental research.

  However, in HASS (humanities, arts and social science), the so-called 'big book' dissertation is more usual. Conventionally, a HASS dissertation is a first attempt at putting together the work that eventually forms your first single-authored book, the essential output for getting an academic job or promotion in this field.

Increasingly, portfolio and hybrid dissertation genres are becoming the norm for all theses.

- The PhD by publication (or 'with publications', 'by compilation' or some other way of saying 'in parts') includes one or more published articles to replace chapters. These are then contextualised and combined through 'framing' chapters (usually an Introduction and combined discussion chapter).
- 'Practice-based' PhDs can include other forms of work in the dissertation, including creative works (a novel, a film, an exhibition), or increasingly other forms of academic practice that might not be best represented in figures, tables or text.

Underneath each of these seemingly different 'genres' is a single concept of a dissertation. There is always an Introduction, with a review of the literature and something about your methods or methodology. Each of these may be a chapter, a section, or maybe just a short paragraph. After that, you have a few chapters where you get into the nitty-gritty research details, maybe results chapters and then a discussion chapter; maybe artefacts and then commentary; or you might combine results and discussion by writing chapters which feature both what you found and what it means twined together. Finally, you should 'pull it all together' in a Conclusion.

A dissertation is a whole work. It must function as an entire entity. The idea behind an IMRAD, big book, portfolio or practice-based dissertation is integrative, it brings these different things together in a way that synthesises, or sets up a dialectic, or constructs an argument (see Chapter 6 for building logical arguments).

A dissertation is not a collection of various separate pieces of writing:

- it is a whole made up of parts;
- it makes a consistent and sustained argument;
- it makes a significant and original contribution to knowledge;
- it does so within the context of a deep and extensive understanding of the field.

Yes, it's complicated, so let's make it visual.

Many students imagine their document as a line of buckets, with the various parts labelled on the front (Figure 7.1).

Your arguments and congruencies won't just 'emerge' or 'be visible' by lining up all the chapters in a row. Nor will they be constructed through the external formatting of having buckets that look the same. Moreover, just tying together these buckets with some string will leave you with . . . a Frankenstein bucket-monster.

What's more, though the buckets might look similar from the outside, once you look more closely, what's going on inside each chapter is complex. Inside a 'case study' bucket, for example, you will have an intro, refer to relevant prior information, discuss material, tie them together into an argument, and a conclusion. You will have sections of close analysis, and sections of big picture argument. You will have parts that link to the rest of the dissertation, and parts that link to the rest of the scholarship. You might even have each of these things in a single paragraph . . . this sounds even worse. We've gone from a bucket monster to a sand monster . . .

You need to imagine a structure beyond the buckets: to think about your dissertation as a whole work. This can be difficult because the dissertation

Figure 7.1 Why chapters are not quite like content 'buckets'

genre requires lots of sections and attributes we don't look for in publications. In Chapter 6, we described the dissertation as a kind of driving test where you have to prove that you know what you are doing. You will need a capacious literature review and a painstaking setting out of your methods and theoretical methodology, which you can cut down when you write an article. The dissertation is always an ugly and hybrid genre, its purpose is to be like an instruction manual of how you got to your conclusions. But it's not okay to think just because the dissertation genre is ugly, you don't have to worry about making a beautiful construction. The dissertation still needs to do its job, and a line of buckets is not going to cut it.

Instead, you can think about your dissertation as a public building, like a hospital. When Inger was a novice architect she had to work on hospital projects, so she knows this design pain intimately. A hospital must be many things to many people. It's got to have rooms to cut people open, rooms to store things, rooms to help people recover, rooms to keep visitors away from people who are recovering, rooms to pray in, and rooms to die. It also needs to be a shopping mall.

And you thought doing a dissertation was hard! A well-designed public building (or dissertation) is the answer to four main questions:

1 What is the purpose of this building? Who is it for and what will they want to do inside it?

2 How do people experience the building? Can they find the front door? Are the corridors wide enough to push two gurneys past each other?

3 Does the final design achieve the outcomes the designer intended? Is one outcome more important than others? If so, does the building achieve the main outcome? A hospital should really be for making sick people better. If it has too many rooms for dying and praying, the designer is sending the wrong message!

4 How does the building work with the other buildings around it? Is it supposed to blend in? Is it supposed to stand out? The Children's Hospital in Melbourne, Australia, is designed to blend with the park and trees behind it and with the other hospital buildings nearby. The hospital was also built as part of a large hospital and medical research precinct, and gains much of its importance and value from being one of a number of similar buildings.

In summary, when putting your dissertation together out of all those bits and pieces:

1 Have the big picture in mind.

2 Think first about your reader's experience.

3 Make sure that even when parts of your document can operate separately, they still work together as a whole.

 (a) It's fine to have a chapter that is really unlike the others, if it's a feature, not a weird annex that looks like you tacked it on when you ran out of budget.

4 Might different readers take different paths through your document?
   (a) Can your reader 'walk the wrong' way through the dissertation and still have the right experience?
5 Does the reader leave the dissertation with the feeling that you knew what you were doing, even if they didn't like it?

Dissertations, like hospitals, can be confronting, boring, frustrating places, but if they do their job well, you leave feeling better than when you came in.

7.2 Turning an annotated bibliography on steroids into a proper literature review

Many students get a lot of negative feedback on their first attempt at a literature review. Common criticisms include 'this is a list', 'there is no through line' or 'an annotated bibliography is not a lit review'. Ouch! The literature review does a lot of work in a dissertation. It forms an essential part of the overall argument, demonstrating credibility, positioning, as well as assembling your academic network (see Chapter 2). However, it typically has two significant life-stages: the initial version, and the final version.

Your first attempt at writing the literature review might look like an 'annotated bibliography on steroids', as Katherine's friend Aleks calls them; a list of books and articles you have read, what you think of them, and how they relate to your thesis. An annotated bibliography on steroids should at least show you have read and understood the field, but it will not be examination-ready yet. In this section, we offer a few practical strategies for developing your reading list into a literature review chapter.

Like so much of the research writing process, a literature review consists of multiple stages and tasks, perhaps spread over multiple years. There is so much literature available, even in niche fields; you won't be able to 'read everything in your field' and 'be up to date', even if you spent most of your time reading. Reviewing the literature is an iterative process. The first time you 'do a lit review' you have to find the resources, read them, take notes, understand difficult concepts, map the field – all before you even sit down to write your first draft. Many books and workshops on reviewing the literature are in fact about this stage. As you beef these reviews up, you may start including more detail from the books, engaging more closely with their arguments.

The initial stage of the process is complete when you have convinced your advisors – and yourself – that you have done enough research and reading around to be confident in your claim of originality and contribution to the field. Everyone has a nightmare story of someone who hasn't done this, like the MA student Katherine studied with in the UK who was planning to do his dissertation on Graham Greene and Catholicism because he didn't think there was much written on it. When he finally started his literature review (very late in the semester), he quickly learned just how wrong he was – leading to a swift rewriting of his research proposal.

The second draft of the review is often more structured and will perhaps have more of an argument. However, a literature review written during the first year will reflect your first-year skills and understanding. By the time the dissertation is ready to be submitted, your understanding of the field and your project should have developed exponentially. So too will your skills of writing, constructing an argument and integrating evidence in a sophisticated way. Most people find they have to extensively rewrite the literature review section, or sections, before submitting the final dissertation.

Practical suggestions for revising your annotated bibliography on steroids into a literature review

1 Know what your original contribution turned out to be

When you start your final rewrite, you should know what your original contribution turned out to be (rather than what you hypothesised it would be as part of your research design). You are now a world expert in your method and area of specialisation. You should be sure about what your theory brings to your evidence, or what your analysis says about your experiments. (You might not feel confident, but you must act confident anyway, see Chapter 6 for a reminder.) As you go back through every section and chapter of the literature sections, review the topic sentences, introductory sections and signposting to check that you are claiming you are writing about the very thing you ended up proving. You may find that aspects of your final arguments and positions aren't covered in the literature you wrote about in the first year; theories mentioned in the lit review might end up being less useful than you initially thought and so can be removed or relegated to a footnote. (See Chapter 2 for more on footnotes, and Chapter 4 for more on signposting, topic sentences and other re-structuring advice.)

2 You now know much more about the field and the other scholars in the field

If your field is populated by other scholars researching and writing and thinking, your final lit review must include research that has come out since your first survey. You also know things you picked up from conferences and following them on Twitter, like which ideas are out of fashion and the various academic tribal feuds. Katherine rephrased a lot of her final draft to avoid offending senior scholars with whom she only partially agreed, but who had a reputation for not holding back on attacking scholars who were on the 'wrong' side of particular arguments. (Yes, this is vague, she might want to publish in that field again one day.)

3 Demonstrate your prior knowledge in the literature section

The structure, content and argument of the rest of the dissertation now exists. What you need to demonstrate in the literature section is prior knowledge so people reading your dissertation can follow you. This advice may seem kind of basic, but you'd be amazed how often we read a dissertation and we're in Chapter 5 and we find ourselves scribbling in the margins, 'WHY ARE YOU ONLY TELLING ME THIS NOW? THIS MATTERED!' Unlike a detective novel, superhero movie, or even a good joke, don't hold back on the punchline. Give it to us upfront.

4 The literature review material might not belong in a single chapter

In HASS dissertations and dissertation by publication, it is common to find literature review work spread out through the whole document. You might structure the lit review as a section in the Introduction and then include more in the introduction to each chapter. Or there might be an overall general review combined with a background section with specific mini-reviews; or some context chapters using extant secondary literature; with archives and primary sources in the remaining chapters. The initial lit review you wrote for confirmation might now be in a dozen little pieces. Check that they all work and cover everything we've listed here. Check for repetition; use cross-references if possible to avoid a boring re-hash of information available elsewhere.

You might do all of this, but your advisor tells you it is still no good. This happens a lot – we understand the frustration. To check that your literature review is 'scholarly', consider if it fits the PRACIS model. This is a model that Katherine has developed to help doctoral students: is it Proportionate, Relevant, Analytical, Critical, Informative and Synthesised?

Writing a PRACIS Literature Review

Proportionate

Are important texts and ideas covered in more extensive detail than unimportant ones? 'Important' will depend on the field and the task at hand. There might, for instance, be a major scholar whose work you are not using: you should at least acknowledge the absence and say why. You might focus on one little article that has been overlooked by everyone else, but which has incredible significance to your work – say why! Katherine's PhD cited a lot of other people's footnotes, appendixes and endnotes. These were things other people thought didn't need to be in the main text of their work, but Katherine was able to demonstrate value. Inger made space for medieval scholarship on guilds in her dissertation on hand gestures because her work was directed at educators, not hand gesture scholars.

Relevant

Is everything in the lit review related to your research and contemporary debates? Or is it a list of absolutely everything you read in your PhD? Avoid the temptation to show the teacher everything you read. As a rule of thumb, secondary research should be less than two decades old, but be sure to check what is 'normal' in your field. In Higher Education research, 30-year-old research can count as current, and in theoretical physics, anything more than a few years old is out of date. Obviously, it's contingent on the project – Plato and Einstein still have something to contribute to some contemporary dissertations!

Analytical

Don't just tell us who said it, when they said it, and what they said. Examiners and advisors want to know how they created their knowledge, why they created it, whether it is relevant to your work, in what ways and to what extent it is relevant (and in what ways and to what extent it isn't relevant).

Critical

Critical doesn't mean disagreeing, or even saying why you agree or disagree. As we highlighted in Chapter 6, significant questions need to be addressed, such as: why did the researcher write this way? What invisible aspects of the research have been assumed and elided? How reliable are their analyses? What assumptions did they make that might have biased their data?

Informative

While a literature review deals with material that is already known, it doesn't mean that your readers will be familiar with it. Particularly for interdisciplinary or mixed methods research, your readers are likely to be somewhat more comfortable in one area than another. A well-written literature review not only shows that the student has read widely, but it also helps the reader to fill in gaps in their understanding or to see what articles they might need to download and read before trying to give feedback. See Chapter 3, and later in this chapter, for more on working across disciplines.

Synthesised

An annotated bibliography on steroids is a list with some signposting. The classic sign that a person has not moved beyond this stage is when there is one paragraph to each book or article (give or take). Synthesis brings the texts together. Perhaps you can group a whole school of thinkers into one paragraph, and account for their limitations and relevance together. Perhaps you have found a thread of similar ideas in quite distinct thinkers. Perhaps a tiny source requires a page or two to explain it fully. Perhaps, when mixed with the special sauce of your insights or a new theoretical lens, some dull old scholars take on a shiny new rainbow life. Section 7.3 talks specifically about a synthesising technique.

7.3 Making and using a literature review matrix

One of the biggest problems with the literature review in any project is there is so much to read. Knowledge? You're soaking in it. Maybe drowning. In Section 7.2, we talked about how to make sure your review of the literature was not just a list of things you read, but something critical and analytical. In this section, we look at some practical steps before you start writing, to structure your notes and then organise yourself to produce more critical and analytical paragraphs.

One of the most common complaints about a literature review section is that it is a 'whistle-stop tour' through a whole lot of stuff that was written before, with no argument gluing it together. It's very hard feedback to respond to because coherence is at both the overall structural level and the granular sentence level. It's a bit like putting a jigsaw together – to get to beautiful overall coherence, it's best to arrange the pieces in clumps: edges, sky, sea, mountain.

Most people neglect the 'clumping' part of the process, but this is when all the best thinking is done – the thinking that enables you to find what editors call the 'red line' that ties it all together. When we say 'thinking', you might have a mental picture of staring into space, tapping a pencil gently against your brow. While that is thinking, it's also a bit like daydreaming. Consider turning your thinking into concrete processes or actions to make it more efficient and effective.

The literature and sources matrix (Table 7.1) is a tool to help bring the material in your thesis together to tell a story: what is technically called 'synthesising'. A matrix is essentially a grid that you can adapt to explore the connections between different pieces of literature, studies, material objects or other sources. We want to acknowledge Jenn from the 'My Studious Life' blog who first wrote about this technique (2011).

Simply put, a literature review matrix is a table with one set of things on the top and another set down the side.

- The top row should reflect the sources (in the case below, different imaginary papers).
- The rows can be anything you like: themes, questions, time periods. Whatever works. In this example, we have used themes.
- Each cell of the matrix represents the intersection between the heading on the column and the heading on the row. The empty cell is an opportunity for you to write a bit of text about the thing or source listed in the top row that is a response to the question, provocation or theme in the row header.

We have used themes in Table 7.1.

Deciding what to put in the left-hand side of the matrix is up to you: you can identify themes before you start reading so that you always know what you are reading for, or develop them as you go. The cell format gives you a small space to write so that you can take notes with more purpose. If you are using the

Table 7.1   Literature review matrix

Themes in research about PhD students	Humbug et al. (2009)	Mewburn (2012)	Whathisname (2013)
Reasons for undertaking a higher degree	Argues the reason why people take up PhD study varies by discipline	Argues that there is a clear gender division in the discipline enrolments	Doesn't mention this this at all – actually, none of the rest of the papers I read did, so I didn't bother following up on this theme any further
Completion rates	Shows that men drop out more than women in almost all disciplines	Shows that older people who are enrolled part-time are more persistent than those younger who enrol part-time	Shows that attrition varies by institution and that the 'richer' institutions lose less students
Social learning in PhD student communities	Doesn't mention this	Shows examples of conversations to show that older people have more complex discussions about 'meta' issues in PhD study than younger students	Doesn't mention this
Relationship with supervisor – how important is it?	Argues that the relationship with supervisor is a key determinant of success	Argues that older people deal with poor supervision better than younger people	Suggests that poorer institutions have a 'younger' supervisor profile

matrix to do a synthesis of literature, it is helpful to arrange the papers by date, with earliest on the left and latest on the right, so that you also generate a timeline of what has been discovered about that topic over time.

You can use the matrix to make reading more productive and serve as a handy 'look-up' table while you are writing. Every time you interrupt your writing to scratch around finding your notes or the original paper to reference, it's easy to lose your train of thought and get distracted. Theoretically, you can string together the text in each row of your matrix to make a paragraph. In practice, it's a bit more complicated. There are many possible sentences you could write along the top row of our fake matrix, but a basic one would look something like this:

> Attrition can be related to the reason people choose to undertake a PhD in the first place. Not many scholars pay attention to the reasons why students are motivated to enrol in a PhD. Two notable exceptions are Humbug et al. (2009) and Mewburn (2012). Humbug et al. showed that different disciplines report very different reasons for beginning a PhD. Mewburn confirmed Humbug et al.'s findings in work in her study of older students, but highlighted the ways that gender further complicated the picture of motivation.

The matrix helped us make a claim about all the literature ('not many scholars') and to highlight the scholars who have bothered to look at this aspect. Arranging our authors by column enabled us to talk about the connection between two authors – even if they didn't refer to each other. This 'connective writing' is pure literature review gold, which makes you seem totally in charge of your field.

A matrix is extremely useful when you are working with a lot of different sources of information. Although it can be time-consuming to make a matrix, it is a good investment of time for busy and part-time dissertation writers. If you are often interrupted in the writing process, the matrix can serve as a way to 'freeze' thinking so that you can pick up where you left off.

Inger finds this process much more effective than writing notes in a journal; it is the only way she ever takes notes when reading. Inger is such a matrix super-fan, she makes historians who come to Thesis Boot Camp make one before they attend. People find it greatly reduces the 'transaction costs' in writing – and they don't have to tote piles of books around. Looking up a reference or thing by date can make fact checking a lot quicker, something historians may appreciate. (A caveat: Katherine regularly co-authors with a historian, and using a visual matrix with tiny cells would be deeply frustrating for his work. As always, all our advice needs testing against your individual situation!) A matrix can also work for anyone to organise the literature section of a chapter. Many science students use a similar model.

If you put the matrix in the Cloud, it can be an excellent tool for co-authoring, enabling you to split up the reading while keeping track of the progress. Inger has used this technique to manage teams of writers of up to six people on a paper – the empty cells show where someone is not pulling their weight!

A matrix is useful at the early stages of writing for finding connections and constructing arguments, but it can be used any time to clarify the 'conversation' you want to have with your sources. The silences are as important as the text – if you find yourself unable to fill in a cell, it's a gap in a paper that can be critiqued. A whole row of silence is the invitation to write a dissertation because it indicates a serious gap in the literature.

7.4 How to write an abstract

An abstract is not just a short version of your dissertation. It's not a summary, or even a blurb – even though it should summarise your work. Your abstract is a specific genre of academic writing that exists to 'sell' your work to potential readers and examiners.

The best abstracts demonstrate the 'moves' (or academic actions) that your piece of writing is going to take and help a reader to identify if your work is relevant to them. In this section, we adapt advice from Kamler and Thompson, in particular, their excellent 'Tiny Texts' concept written for students in HASS disciplines (2012, 2014). In this section, we adapt their 'Five Moves' template for use by research students in science writing and beyond.

The Tiny Text concept recognises that the academic abstract is a mini-genre, a tiny microcosm of your thesis as a whole. Rather than try to boil your dissertation down to its essence in a sort of radical stock-making reduction, a Tiny Text magically extracts its power. So, come with us; pick up your wand and follow these five 'academic moves' and create your own Tiny Text. Each 'move' is about one sentence long for chapters, conference proposals, articles; you might need a few sentences for each move if you are writing a Tiny Text for a book or dissertation.

Using an example, again completely made up, we show you how to adapt the five 'moves' into the kinds of sentences you would see in STEM, HASS and creative theses. All disciplines follow the pattern: (1) Locate; (2) Focus; (3) Anchor; (4) Report; (5) Argue; and (6) Show Significance, but the ways they do it might involve different strategies.

Okay, so let's say you have discovered a magical unicorn hair. Awesome. Now the uses of unicorn hair are many and various. But this is your unicorn hair, and you want to use it to lay the ghosts of the ravening pirates – thus you use the unicorn hair in your own series of ritualised moves.

The first move is Locate

Locate your work in a wider academic debate by writing a sentence that shows you are responding to, developing or reacting to other scholars helps position your current research. Take the following, totally made up, examples:

> *STEM*: Recent studies suggest that dissolving unicorn hair in fairy acid is effective in laying Viking ghosts (Harald, 2013; Erik, 2015; Redbeard, 2015), and using it for pirate ghosts has been proposed as theoretically possible (Harr, 2015; Hearty, 2016; Rumm, 2017a).
>
> *HASS*: While scholars like Cutlass (1988) have declared that unicorns are 'no longer relevant' in ghost studies, the cultural context of unicorn hair in pirate ghost rituals has been explored by scholars influenced by Louise Pegleg's foundational anthropological monograph, *Unicorns and Ghosts* (1987) for the last three decades.[1]

[1]See further Doubloon (2012); Polly (1991); Topsail (1995, 1998).

Creative theses: Using Tvinkl's theory of reflective practice (1962, 1967), the project 'Ahoy there, unicorn hair!' can be understood as . . .

As the creative example shows, the move can just be a clause, rather than a whole sentence. If the field is divided in an acrimonious battle between unicorn hair advocates and detractors, you might need two sentences and a footnote, like the HASS example.

Your second move is Focus

What, specifically, will your thesis address? This is a sentence that explains exactly where your thesis sits in this wider field of research and/or debate. Zoom into your specific topic. Your research question might be useful here!

STEM: We test the efficacy of unicorn hair to lay pirate ghosts.
HASS: This dissertation explores five eighteenth-century case studies to ask whether unicorn hair had practical or symbolic meaning for practitioners.
Creative: I created site-specific woven works which interrogate the historical and supernatural narratives around unicorn hair and ghosts.

The third move is to Anchor

This is where you introduce your lens or method. Anchoring your work means you sink down roots in well-recognised ways of researching in your discipline.

STEM: The study dissolved 4 unicorn hairs in 10% solution of fairy acid and applied 10ml of liquid to level 3, level 7, and level 10 pirate ghost hauntings in three sites in Cornwall.
HASS: This dissertation undertakes a close textual analysis of five published diaries by magic practitioners based near Portsmouth between 1700 *and* 1800.
Creative: I will document a practice-led research project into making nets woven out of unicorn hair and place them in venues with reported incidences of pirate ghost haunting across the UK.

The fourth move is Report

What are your data findings? This line is often left out of abstracts, but is so useful for the reader. Remember: no-one wants to be surprised in academic writing. We are not in a reality TV show here; don't save up the good stuff for a big reveal later. Lay it all out now.

STEM: We find that 10ml is effectual in banishing pirate ghosts for level 3 hauntings, but that at level 7 and higher, 10ml only produces moderate fading.

HASS: The journals reveal that unicorn hair was not simply instrumental for the practitioners, but had a range of religious meanings which developed from purity and virginity symbols in the earlier part of the century, to sacrificial symbols from 1775.

Creative: The outcome of my project has been an exhibition, presenting my project's findings through a repetition of the net making within the Institution art gallery space, using digital 'ghosts' and recordings to recreate the coastal environment.

What counts as data, and what counts as a finding, are very much specific to your discipline and your methodology. In practice-based research or hybrid creative-critical theses, an artwork may be the 'finding'.

Your next move is Argue

Your argument can usually be summed up as the answer to your research question.

STEM: We hypothesise that the volume of unicorn hair is significant in addressing the level of hauntings, and that increasing the volume of unicorn hair used would lead to successful laying of ghosts at levels 7 and above.

HASS: This research suggests that changes in the cultural meaning of unicorn hair parallel changes seen in literary texts and artistic representations.

Creative: The PhD takes up the operational analogy of the spider web, a construction that collects insects and uses them as a source of food, as a parallel for how unicorn nets might intervene in, transform, and re-circulate ghosts in coastal areas.

Finally, you need to show the Significance

This is the most important stage if your aim is to get this paper accepted in a journal or conference. What does this original knowledge you have created add to the field? Don't forget the true value of your dissertation isn't actually what you found out, it's what other people can do with it.

STEM: This study is the first experimental study of the use of unicorn hair in laying pirate ghosts, which importantly replicates the findings for Viking ghosts of Harald (2013) in a new population.

HASS: The five journals importantly help us to fill a gap in the scholarship between maritime ghost studies in the seventeenth (Doubloon, 2012) and nineteenth centuries (Polly, 1991).

Creative: This is the first study to discuss unicorn hair weaving in the context of pirate ghosts for a creative practice audience.

Now you know what to look for, collect journals for your area and dissect their abstracts. As you go, think about which ones interested you and which ones seemed dull or unhelpful. You'll notice there are some standard ways of introducing these moves in your discipline and some people have neat ways to achieve the same thing with a bit of extra sparkle. Steal their magical moves and practise making them your own.

A well-written abstract, or Tiny Text can be useful before you have even written the work. The Tiny Text is a great planning tool for doing a lot of hard thinking work before you write your first sentence. Katherine finds that a conference proposal written as a Tiny Text is much more likely to be accepted and easier to turn into a presentation. She finds this technique so useful at every stage of academic writing that she has saved a quick version of this section on her phone so she can always introduce someone to the concept – and emails it on to a researcher at least every couple of months.

7.5 How to write a good glossary

There are lots of descriptions about what a glossary is, but it's hard to find good advice about how to make one. On the face of it, a glossary is a simple list of key terms and short descriptions of these terms, designed to help the reader understand complex or unfamiliar language. A glossary is usually alphabetical, and our advice is to follow convention in this case (it's a useful tool, not a conversation piece). A useful glossary is an excellent navigation tool for the reader, but a great one also serves a rhetorical purpose. By 'rhetorical' we mean it affects the reader, it makes them feel something about you, the writer; specifically, that a knowledgeable, competent scholar is in charge. If you can achieve this effect, you have accomplished part of the complex task of getting a reader on your side, which, as we have repeatedly stressed, is critical to your work getting a sympathetic reception from an academic audience.

Let's go back to first principles for a moment: what exactly is a glossary? Where did it come from? What did the first ones look like?

What is a glossary?

Glossary starts life as a Latin loan-word from the ancient Greek word for 'tongue' or language, used to talk about a rare, foreign or difficult term that needs explanation. 200 years later, in Late Antiquity, it starts to mean the explanation itself, rather than the word, and 200 years later, in Medieval Latin, it becomes plural and stands for a collection of 'glosses' put together as a glossary. The best-known 'glossators' (as people who wrote glossaries were called) were not just writing simple comments or summaries of texts, but full commentaries, translations, or legal opinions. The glossator was a special kind of expert who made that rare, foreign or difficult knowledge available to the ordinary reader.

This history tells us a glossary is not just a collection of key terms that you use in your dissertation, summarised for the reader, but something that makes your text more accessible, approachable and authoritative.

A step-by-step guide to producing a glossary

1 Do you need a glossary?

Decide if you need a glossary or not. We would argue that you only need one if it's going to be of genuine use to the reader. Start by asking yourself a series of questions:

- Are you using a lot of terms not common in your field or area?
- Is your project cross-disciplinary? Do you import concepts or methods from elsewhere?
- Are you using multiple terms to mean similar things?
- Are some terms very similar in spelling and/or construction and thus potentially confusing?
- Are you using many acronyms?
- Are there places, people or things that reoccur and need to be explained? (You can include different kinds of glossaries for this, for instance, a biographical index or list of places.)

If you answered 'yes' to most of these questions, your dissertation would benefit from a glossary.

2 Which terms will you include?

Selection of which terms to include is critical. A glossary should demystify terms for the reader, not state the bleeding obvious. There's no point in providing descriptions for a whole bunch of common terms; your reader will feel like you are talking down to them.

It's vitally important to realise that you are not the best person to identify what needs to go in the glossary. If you have been working on a research project for a long time, there is no doubt you will be suffering from the Curse of Knowledge. The Curse of Knowledge is when you've forgotten what it's like not to know what you know. We suggest you ask a colleague or fellow student (not your advisor – they have the Curse of Knowledge as well) to read your whole text and underline words they don't immediately understand.

This 'cold reader' process will give you a starter list. Reading the whole text of a dissertation and identifying words is a considerable investment of time. We suggest you team up: offer to swap texts with another student and perform the duty for each other.

3 What is your potential 'cross-over' readership?

Think about your potential 'cross-over' readership. We'll have much more to say about that in Section 7.6 on multidisciplinary work, but every good academic writer should assume that people with different disciplinary experiences will encounter their work.

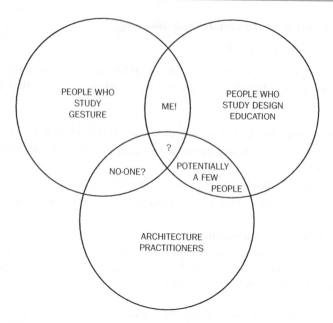

Figure 7.2 A Venn diagram of audiences for Inger's dissertation

Table 7.2   Identifying the audiences for Inger's dissertation

Reader	What they already know	What they probably don't know
Gesture scholars	'Prosody'	ANT
Design studio teachers		'Prosody', ANT
Practitioners		'Prosody', ANT
Education scholars	ANT	

In order to make your writing accessible, you want all your likely readers to be able to understand your work. In order to do that, you need to define your audience.

One way to start defining the audience for the writing is to use a Venn diagram (Figure 7.2) to name potential readers and see where they 'cross over' each other's areas.

4 Sort your terms according to audiences

Start to sort the various terms you have identified into a table. The above is a table that Inger could have produced from her Venn diagram (Table 7.2). You can see that some terms are understood and others are not. The value of using a table is to brainstorm in a structured way.

5 Succinctly explain your terms

We'll assume you are capable of producing text about the word definitions, so we're not going to outline this part in any detail. The challenge here is to keep it short. Try to boil down to a couple of sentences at most. Expect this to take a few goes – and maybe look up some of the sections on writing concisely in Chapters 4 and 5.

6 Where will you put the glossary?

Where would the glossary go? We think it depends a bit on length. Shorter glossaries can go at the start, long ones might be an appendix or a combination of both.

Be creative! Your readers will thank you.

7.6 Structuring multidisciplinary work

If you have read all the other sections of this book, you will realise that working across boundaries involves dealing with more than one 'academic tribe' (see Chapter 3). If you are dealing with multiple academic advisors, each one is likely to have been trained in a slightly (or radically) different system. Their ideas on the norms of language use and what counts as knowledge will vary. You might be asking them to master a whole new academic 'dialect' as well as expose them to unfamiliar ideas and concepts. They will also have different ideas about structuring a dissertation. Earlier in the chapter we addressed the typical genres of dissertations, but here we talk about strategies for defending your interdisciplinary work.

Many academics in the same tribe don't agree with each other, so when you get multiple tribes together . . . well, suffice to say you can find yourself in the middle of a war, where the feedback from each expert contradicts the others. There can be endless demands to reshape the work first to one discipline, then to another. Students can, and have, driven themselves mad trying to please everyone.

Outside of academia, hybrid vigour is often appreciated in all its multifaceted glory. Interdisciplinary research is essential to answering the difficult questions of today – and you can do active work to improve your chances of successfully brokering peace between your disciplinary tribes.

Here are five great ways to structure your multidisciplinary work for success:

1 Have a good Introduction

A good Introduction always matters, but with interdisciplinary research it matters more. Flag that the dissertation will work across numerous disciplines and draw on tools and ideas from all of them. Signalling and signposting will be very important here; include a chapter synopsis so that you guide potential readers through your beautiful interdisciplinary labyrinth.

2 Write for all your audiences

Think about who your different audiences might be. To ensure everyone who might read your work has at least some chance of understanding it, your dissertation should be put together in a way that allows a non-expert at least the option of making sense of technical terms or jargon. Your glossary and use of explanatory footnotes will help (see Chapter 2, and Section 7.5 on glossaries). If necessary, take the time to write an early section that defines key terms, where they have been taken from, and how they will be deployed in the context of this work.

3 You don't have to make all the disciplines happy, all the time

It can help to make up a risk analysis table listing the various audiences and outlining the risks for each chapter. Remember any good risk analysis includes both the likelihood the risk will occur and the severity of the risk. If a particular type of audience is possible, but highly unlikely to encounter the work (or examine it), you might decide not to spend time accommodating their specific needs.

If you're drawing on radically different fields, consider addressing their different approaches in different chapters. Inger had this problem in her own dissertation, which explored how architects gesture while they are designing. When Inger put the results of her two methods together she found they completely contradicted each other. Inger puzzled over this for a year, before deciding to merely present the results separately. In her conclusion, Inger pointed out that it was a well-established premise that each research method produces a different 'reality' and both sets of results were, therefore, true. Although the results were contradictory, they were both useful for different reasons. One examiner loved this explanation, the other was less enthusiastic, but accepted that she had done the analysis properly and made a good argument on philosophical grounds. Mischief managed!

If you are going to separate out content like this, make sure you label these chapters effectively and use the Introduction to signal to the reader where they are and how they are arranged.

4 Can you use a single theory or method to bring all your strands together?

Instead of separating out the content as we discussed in point 3, working across multiple disciplines might be an opportunity to re-frame your work through a single lens. If you do this, you must try to reconcile a combination of facets of approaches from other disciplines via this lens. For example, Katherine wrote her dissertation between musicology and literary studies. While these are significantly different fields, both fields use a model of 'close analysis' and 'cultural history'. Katherine spent a chapter showing (as her original contribution) that these approaches in the two fields could, in fact, be merged productively, which is something that seems obvious to outsiders but is still not settled for experts. Then she went ahead and produced historicist close readings of the music and words of songs together, which formed the basis of the methodology of a later co-authored book and article, so it's still persuading editors and reviewers! Give the reader an understanding of where you position this work within or between the fields it draws on.

Top tip – it's much easier to 'locate' the interdisciplinary work in one discipline and reach into other disciplines for techniques and approaches.

5 Finally, don't forget how important it is to get the reader on your side

Create a compelling argument for why more than one disciplinary approach is needed to investigate the problem at hand. Make it clear that the combination of disciplines chosen is not merely an attempt to be novel – it is the absolute best way to approach the central question of the work.

Go bravely into the interdisciplinary woods friends – and take a map, a light and some friends with you!

8 The end of this book, but not the end of your dissertation

Congratulations, you have finished this book! Maybe you started at the beginning and read all the way through to the end. Maybe you have just ducked in for the one chapter you needed, and are now heading back to the lab or library. Either way, we hope this book has given you enlightenment, encouragement and practical techniques to respond to the typical issues that cause academic writing trouble.

We hope you now have a more sophisticated understanding of the complexities of academic writing. The academic writer must explain new and complicated information to a reader; demonstrate they belong in the academic club; avoid offending (or boring) other academics; conform to the norms of technical academic English; and know when to bend the rules.

If that feels overwhelming, it might also help to remember that a dissertation is not a bridge, or brain surgery, or a poem. No-one will die if you get it wrong. You can get away with the odd waffly sentence, that word that wasn't the best choice, that one muddy paragraph. What's more, you have lots of chances to get it right – or at least make it better. Now you have this book you can look forward to getting feedback, not fear it. With the three of us to help you de-code the frustrating feedback, and the strategies we offer, you can roll up your sleeves and try again.

If you are someone who gives feedback to student writers, we hope you also found this book useful. We know that explaining exactly what is wrong with a piece of writing, and explaining how to fix it, can be really hard. All of us teach academic writing professionally, and even we struggled to make some of the chapters easy to understand (ask us about themes and rhemes some time!). We hope this book also works for you in reverse – when you find yourself writing 'waffle!' or 'uncritical' or 'you don't sound very academic', you might also photocopy a few pages from this book. Telling your student to 'Read this section on how to use footnotes' should save you time, and get you the improved academic writing results you want.

Finally, we want this book to be part of a bigger conversation about how to communicate academic research. Over and over again, we stress that all our advice needs to be applied with judgement. Academic dissertations are changing fast, and the next decade will no doubt bring new changes to how people write, structure, revise, and distribute their work. The three of us will keep reading the new books that come out with recommendations on how to approach these challenges. We'll also continue to explore how to improve our own research and writing strategies, and how to teach them to others. Inger and Katherine will keep blogging. We'd love to hear from you about what works, what improvements you've made, and how you are applying these strategies to new kinds of research that haven't even been invented yet.

With this 'Swiss Army knife' of a multi-tool book in your pocket, go out there and get your dissertation back up and running. Good luck, write well, and change the world! We'll be cheering you on.

Notes

1 UK and Worldwide Thesis Boot Camps page: http://www.petafreestone.com/thesis-boot-camp/
2 Comment supplied by a student, who wishes to remain anonymous, as an example for this book. The end of the story was much happier: '3 months later I passed with no corrections and my examiners' reports stated it was one of the most outstandingly written theses they had ever read.' (Anonymous, web form comment, 16 February 2018).
3 In Australia, the correct way to describe Indigenous individuals is by their language/tribal association, e.g. as a Wiradjuri woman. Wiradjuri people have traditionally lived around what is now central New South Wales, inland from Australia's central east coast.
4 See http://www.vischeck.com/vischeck/vischeckImage.php
5 Too much of Katherine's life was spent trying to work out the science of zombies to write this paragraph. As far as she can see, most zombie writing goes: 'magic gas/science experiment/disease/genetic mutation – look, it's just scary okay???' which is precisely her point.
6 Rhetorical questions are asked without expecting an answer. However, if you ask a question in an academic setting, you may get an answer you don't want! While we were writing this book, we would occasionally tweet screen shots of the text in progress. When one of Inger's colleagues, Catherine Frieman (@CJfrieman), saw our paragraph, she wrote to us with an excellent example of the dangers of the rhetorical question in an academic context: 'I hate rhetorical questions for one very good and personal reason: I once used one in a conf paper one and a hoary old prof stood up, repeated it, answered differently to what I'd intended, then used it to savage my whole paper. Never give a hostile reader such a golden opening, say I.'
Inger disagrees slightly on this point. She loves a rhetorical question, used stylistically, but acknowledges it can make you sound pompous. Rhetorical questions used in undergraduate essays can sound presumptuous (remember we told you how hierarchical academic writing is?). However, if well handled, rhetorical questions can make you sound provocative and challenging. You notice them creeping into the text of some great senior scholars who are getting their grump on. Our advice is, as always: 'handle with care'.
7 We made a very definite statement there but we find ourselves conflicted by the troubling gap that sometimes exists between theory and practice. Powerful academics have been known to stifle dissenters, especially those who are too 'low' in the hierarchy to fight back. Just because you are being squashed doesn't mean your critiques aren't valid – but you might need to be strategic about how and when you make your critical analysis public.
8 Researchers show that when children draw scientists, they are still twice as likely to draw a man as a woman, for example (Miller et al. 2108).
9 Cisgendered: people who identify with their birth-assigned gender. Heterosexual: people who are attracted to people of the opposite sex. LBGTIQ+: lesbian, bisexual, gay, trans, intersex, queer; the plus sign stands in for, at time of writing, another 10 letters denoting different gender identities and sexual preferences.

10 This is one of the best examples in the book of deploying parataxis and hypotaxis (see Chapter 5). One of the reasons to avoid extreme contrasts is that it can make people laugh, which may not be your intention.
11 Hyland (2004) draws our attention to the indeterminacy of academic language use. We refer you to Hyland's excellent work if you want to do a deep dive into the linguistic nerdery of academic dialects, suffice to point out here that skilful use of these expression markers is difficult and will take some time (perhaps a lifetime) to master.

References

Armstrong, J.S. (1980) Unintelligible management research and academic prestige. *Interfaces*, 10(2): 80–6.

Azar, B.S. (2002) *Fundamentals of English Grammar*. Harlow: Longman.

Beardsley, M.C. (1950) *Practical Logic*. Englewood Cliffs, NJ: Prentice-Hall.

Becher, T. and Trowler, P. (2001) *Academic Tribes and Territories: Intellectual Enquiry and the Culture of Disciplines*. Maidenhead: McGraw-Hill Education.

Becker, H.S. (2010) Writing for social scientists: How to start and finish your thesis, book, or article. Available at: www/ReadHowYouWant.com.

Boice, R. (1990) *Professors as Writers: A Self-Help Guide to Productive Writing* Stillwater, OK: New Forums Press.

Booth, W.C., Colomb, G.G. and Williams, J.M. (2003) *The Craft of Research* (2nd edn). Chicago, IL: University of Chicago Press.

De Beauvoir, S. (1949) *Le Deuxième Sex (The Second Sex)*. Paris: Gallimard.

Douglas, J.M., Knox, L., De Maio, C., Bridge, H., Drummond, M. and Whiteoak, J. (2016) Effectiveness of Communication-specific Coping Intervention for adults with traumatic brain injury: preliminary results. *Neuropsychological Rehabilitation*, DOI: 10.1080/09602011.2016.1259114.

Dreyfus, S.E. and Dreyfus, H.L. (1980) A five-stage model of the mental activities involved in directed skill acquisition (No. ORC-80-2). Berkeley, CA: University of California Berkeley, Operations Research Center.

Dunleavy, P. (2014) In a book or PhD, start each chapter cleanly. Never link back. Medium. Available at: https://medium.com/advice-and-help-in-authoring-a-phd-or-non-fiction/in-a-book-or-phd-start-each-chapter-cleanly-never-link-back-3b2865e44173.

Elbow, P. (1998) *Writing Without Teachers*. New York: Oxford University Press.

Firth, K. (2008) The MacNeices and their circles: poets and composers in collaboration 1939–54. PhD thesis, Oxford Brookes University.

Firth, K. (2018) 'The way to learn the music of verse is to listen to it': Ezra Pound's 'The Pisan Cantos' and the 'Sequence of the Musical Phrase'. In K. O'Callaghan (ed.) *Musical Modernism: Essays on Language and Music in Modernist Literature*. London: Routledge, pp. 159–72.

González, V.M. and Mark, G. (2004) Constant, constant, multi-tasking craziness: managing multiple working spheres. In *Proceedings of the SIGCHI Conference on Human Factors in Computing Systems*, April, ACM, pp. 113–20.

Hall, E.T. (1976) *Beyond Culture*. New York: Anchor Books.

Haraway, D.J. (1997) Modest_Witness@Second_Millennium.FemaleMan_Meets_OncoMouse: *Feminism and Technoscience*. Hove: Psychology Press.

Hyland, K. (1998) *Hedging in Scientific Research Articles* (Pragmatics & Beyond New Series, Vol. 54). New York: John Benjamins Publishing.

Hyland, K. (2004) *Disciplinary Discourses*. Ann Arbor, MI: University of Michigan Press.

IMDB (1991) *Star Trek: The Next Generation* (TV Series) in Theory (1991) Whoopi Goldberg: Guinan. Available at: https://www.imdb.com/title/tt0708735/characters/nm0000155

Jenn (2011) Synthesis Matrix for literature review. My Studious Life blog, 16 June. Available at: https://mystudiouslife.wordpress.com/2011/06/16/synthesis-matrix-for-literature-review/

Johnson, S. and Boswell, J. ([1785] 1984) *A Journey to the Western Islands of Scotland and The Journal of a Tour to the Hebrides.* ed. P. Levi. Harmondsworth: Penguin.

Kamler, B. and Thompson, P. (2014) *Helping Doctoral Students Write: Pedagogies for Supervision* (rev. ed.). London: Routledge.

Kiley, M. (2009) Identifying threshold concepts and proposing strategies to support doctoral candidates. *Innovations in Education and Teaching International,* 46(3): 293–304.

King, S. (2002) *On Writing.* New York: Simon & Schuster.

Kumar, A. (2015) *Lunch with a Bigot: The Writer in the World.* Durham, NC: Duke University Press.

Lamott, A. (2007) *Bird by Bird: Some Instructions on Writing and Life.* New York: Anchor Books.

Latour, B. (1993) *We Have Never Been Modern.* Cambridge, MA: Harvard University Press.

Lovitts, B. (2007) *Making the Implicit Explicit: Creating Performance Expectations for the Dissertation.* New York: Stylus.

Mewburn, I. (2009) Constructing bodies: gesture, speech and representation at work in architectural design studios. Dissertation, University of Melbourne.

Mewburn, I. (2011) Troubling talk: assembling the PhD candidate. *Studies in Continuing Education,* 33(3): 321–32.

Mewburn, I., Cuthbert, D. and Tokareva, E. (2014) Experiencing the progress report: an analysis of gender and administration in doctoral candidature. *Journal of Higher Education Policy and Management,* 36(2): 155–71.

Miller, D.I., Nolla, K.M., Eagly, A.H. and Uttal, D.H. (2018) The development of children's gender-science stereotypes: a meta-analysis of 5 decades of US draw-a-scientist studies. *Child Development,* DOI: 10.1111/cdev.13039.

Mullins, G. and Kiley, M. (2002) 'It's a PhD, not a Nobel Prize': How experienced examiners assess research theses. *Studies in Higher Education,* 27(4): 369–86, DOI: 10.1080/0307507022000011507.

Nakamura, J. and Csikszentmihályi, M. (2001) Flow: theory and research. In C.R. Snyder, E. Wright and S.J. Lopez (eds) *Handbook of Positive Psychology.* Oxford: Oxford University Press, pp. 195–206.

Nakata, M.N. (2007) *Disciplining the Savages, Savaging the Disciplines.* Melbourne: Aboriginal Studies Press.

Pitt, R. and Mewburn, I. (2016) Academic superheroes? A critical analysis of academic job descriptions. *Journal of Higher Education Policy and Management,* 38(1): 88–101, DOI: 10.1080/1360080X.2015.1126896

Silva, P.J. (2007) *How to Write a Lot.* Washington, DC: American Psychological Association.

Smith, L.T. (2013) *Decolonizing Methodologies: Research and Indigenous Peoples.* London: Zed Books.

Sobel, D. (2017) *The Glass Universe: How the Ladies of the Harvard Observatory Took the Measure of the Stars.* Harmondsworth: Penguin.

Sutton, R.I. and Shaw, B.M. (1995) What theory is not. *Administrative Science Quarterly,* 40(3): 371–84. Available at: http://haas.berkeley.edu/faculty/papers/stawtheory.pdf

Swift, K. and Miller, C. (1995) *The Handbook of Non-sexist Writing for Writers, Editors and Speakers.* New York: Women's Press.

Sword, H. (2012a) Zombie nouns. *The New York Times,* 23 July.

Sword, H. (2012b) *Stylish Academic Writing.* Cambridge, MA: Harvard University Press.

Thompson, P. and Kamler, B. (2012) *Writing for Peer Reviewed Journals: Strategies for Getting Published.* London: Routledge.

van Gelder, T. (2015) Using argument mapping to improve critical thinking skills. In M. Davies and R. Barnett (eds) *The Palgrave Handbook of Critical Thinking in Higher Education*. New York: Palgrave Macmillan, pp. 183–92.

Wallace, A.R. (1869) *The Malay Archipelago: The Land of the Orang-Utan and the Bird of Paradise; A Narrative of Travel, with Studies of Man and Nature*. London: Courier Corporation Press.

Wisker, G. and Robinson, G. (2013) Doctoral 'orphans': nurturing and supporting the success of postgraduates who have lost their supervisors. *Higher Education Research & Development*, 32(2): 300–13.

Zinsser, W. (1983) *On Writing Well*. New York: Harper & Row.

Index

Ableism 113
Abstract 144–47
Academic dialect(s) 4, 13, 46, 88–9, 151, 157
Academicese 12–13, 18
Adjectives 37, 95–97, 104
Adverbs 15, 37, 49–52, 67
Annotated bibliography 138–9, 141
Appendix 33, 35–6, 100, 140, 151
Argument 35–55, 58, 65, 67–9, 71, 77–9, 82, 86
Argument diagramming 122–27, 105–7, 118, 122–53

Barbara Lovitts 19
Beardsley, M.C 123–24
Becher and Trowler 13, 24
Becker, Howard 64, 95
Blogging 5, 155
Boice, Robert 77–8
Boosters 121
Booth et al 44, 46–8
Brick wall, as metaphor 76
Bruno Latour 20

Car driving as metaphor 4, 51, 69, 118
Chapters 66, 76, 79, 81–7, 92, 134–6, 140, 145, 152–4
Clarity 15, 33, 53–4, 59, 89, 92
Class 12, 26–7, 35, 112–16, 121
Clause 15, 49, 64–5, 70, 98–9, 146
Cleverness 116–119
Coherence 51, 59, 68, 142
Colonialism 115
Conference drinks party, as metaphor 31
Conjunctive adverbs 37, 49–52, 67
Courtrooms, as a metaphor 28, 47, 130
Critique table 107
Cutting words 99

Deduction 130–31
Descriptive 21, 53, 105, 108
Diagrams 36, 52, 59, 79, 105, 123, 127–8
Dissertation types 6, 14, 21, 65, 111, 134–5, 150

Doctoral orphans 47–8
Dreyfus and Dreyfus learning framework 4
Driving, as a metaphor 4, 51, 118, 137
Dunleavy, Patrick 55

Editing 11, 29, 58–9, 67–9, 75–9, 85–7, 91–2, 101, 110
Hall, Edward 59
Epistemologies 39
Exploratory vs explanatory writing 43

Fencing, as a metaphor 12, 18, 28, 120
Figures 36–7, 52–5, 135
Filler words 15, 99, 101–4
First draft 41, 76–8, 87, 90, 93, 110, 138, 162
Flow 33–5, 58, 70, 75–9, 86, 90, 102, 118, 127–9
Footnotes 35–6, 40, 100, 139–40, 152–54, 30–4
Francisco Cirillo 8

Gender 22, 38–9, 80, 113
Gender, in writing 113–4, 156
Generative writing 76–9
Germanic words 16–17, 26, 60, 64
Glossary 33, 40, 134, 148–52
Grammar 2–4, 37, 72, 76, 89, 92–3, 98–9

HASS 21–3, 135, 140, 145
Hedging terms 102, 119–22, 131–2
High and low context languages 33
High School 4–5, 13, 19
High Table dinner, as a metaphor 12
Hospital, as a metaphor for the dissertation 137–8
How to write a sentence 62
Hypotaxis 97–9
Hypothesis driven research stories 41–3

I (use of subjective pronouns) 110–1
Identity work 3
IMRAD 135–6
Induction 131

Interdisciplinary 34, 38–41, 141
Introductions 14–15, 32, 43, 58, 67–9,
    74, 78, 81, 92, 111, 135, 140, 151
Indigenous 26, 114–5, 156
Invasion, England 12

Jargon 2, 18–20, 64, 116–9, 152
Jigsaw puzzle, as a metaphor 43, 142, 162

Kamler and Thompson 3, 81, 145, 162
Hyland, K 22, 24–5, 27, 157–8
King, Stephen 95

Lamott, A 77
Latinate words 64, 162
LBGTIQ+ 114, 156, 162
Liam Connell 10
Literature review 22, 27, 78, 81, 91, 117–8,
    105, 134–44
Literature review matrix 141–44
Logic 77–8, 86, 106–9, 122–6, 130–31
Logical argumentation 13–18, 106, 162

Manchester academic phrase bank 121
Maybe later file 100
Middle class dinner party, as a metaphor
    12, 26, 48–9, 119–120
Multi–tasking 66, 91
Multidisciplinary work 30, 149, 151–2
My studious life blog 142, 158

Nominalisations 95–7
Note taking 9, 36, 76, 78, 80, 134, 138,
    142–44, 144

Object 92–5
Oxbridge 12

Paragraph construction 46
Paragraph length 65
Parataxis 64, 97–9
Passive voice 89, 92–5, 109, 63
Perfect sentence vortex 90–1
Peta Freestone 10
Phrase book 40
Planning 76–9, 81–5, 91, 148
Politeness 26
Pomodoro technique 8–9, 77, 91
Posse, as a metaphor 12
POWER cycle 91
Power relations 19, 112–5, 156

PRACIS (proportionate, relevant,
    analytical, Critical, informative,
    synthesised) 140
Professional writing/reports 2, 4, 91
Proust 62

Quilt as metaphor 76

Race 114–5
Rachael Cayley 49, 86
Reading 4, 9, 13, 15–19, 30, 34, 37, 46, 60,
    67–8, 87, 91, 98, 112, 117, 138–49
Reading, skimming 67
Red line 143
References, As talismans 12
References, As witnesses 28
Reflexive doubt 106–9
Reflexivity (with the subjective I) 110–11
Reverse Outline 59, 69, 86–91
Rewriting 87
Rhemes 70–78
Rhetorical questions 156

Scholarly 26, 60–1, 96, 102, 105–20, 140
Scholastic methods, medieval 18
Self–citation 32
Self–plagiarism 32
Sentence Clauses 15, 64–5, 98
Sentence Length 97–8
Sentences 4, 14–17, 37, 44–9, 58, 61–79,
    89–95, 97–9, 110–11, 139, 143, 145
Sexism 113
Shitty first draft 77
Shut Up and Write 7–10
Signpost language 14, 49–58, 67–9, 75, 81,
    102, 139, 141, 152
Snowflake outline 81–85
Spider Diagrams 79–81, 123–29
STEM 22, 135, 145–47
Strike through tool 99–100
Structure 14, 41, 44, 51–3, 58–62, 66–71,
    76–8, 85–8, 93–4, 134–42, 151–55
Stuffing words 102
Style 1–5, 13–16, 23–32, 35, 55, 59–62,
    76–7, 101–2, 110
Sub–vocalising 98
Subject 63–6, 92–5
Subordinate clause 98–9, 130

Tables 36, 40, 52–55, 107, 135
Taglines 66–7

Tense, past and present 72, 75
Tenses, mixing 72, 74
Themes and Rhemes 78–81
Theory, in writing 20
Thesis 'buckets' structure 136
Thesis Boot Camp 7, 9–11, 43, 77, 91,144
Thesis Map 79–83
Time boxing 8
Tiny texts 145
Topic Sentences 14, 44–6, 65–9
Transaction costs 144
Translated material, presentation 34

Van Gelder, T 123–4
Verb Cheat Sheet 26–7
Verb Types 12, 17, 24–6

Verbs, Evaluative 24–6
Verbs, Passive Aggressive 26
Verbs, Signalling Belonging 25
vision impairment 53

Waffle 89, 121, 154
Warrants 37, 145–9
Wiradjuri 156
Wisker and Robinson 47
Word count 89, 109, 101–2
Writing productivity 8–10, 129–30
Writing Retreats 9–11
Writing Cycle 91

Zinsser, William 101
Zombie words 95–97